1000
beads

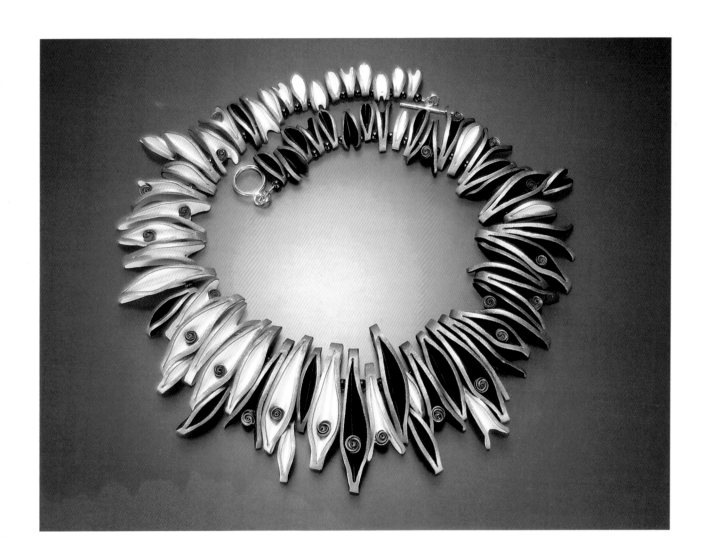

1000
beads

Kristina Logan, Juror

LARK
CRAFTS
Asheville

SENIOR EDITOR
Julie Hale

DESIGNER
Michelle Owen

FRONT COVER, CLOCKWISE FROM LEFT
Lynne Glazzard
Aqua Spiral Enameled Bead, 2012

Ingeborg Vandamme
Landscape, 2013

Floriane Lataille
Tricot, 2011

Barbara Simon
Info Beads, 2009

BACK COVER, CLOCKWISE FROM
MAIN IMAGE
Cynthia Toops
Tubes, 2012

Jason Morrissey
*Secret Language of
Birthdays Bead*, 2007

Karmen Schmidt
Flights of Fancy, 2013

Carol Blackburn
Tetra Beads, 2012

Tracey Broome
Raku Beads, 2012

SPINE
Patty Lakinsmith
Bead from the Reptilian Series, 2011

FRONT FLAP
Janet Graff
Gears Around, 2012

BACK FLAP
Ann Klem
Faceted Cubes, 2013

TITLE PAGE
Wiwat Kamolpornwijit
Rose Petals, 2013

OPPOSITE
Barbara Paz
Primo Necklace, 2012

LARK CRAFTS

An Imprint of Sterling Publishing
387 Park Avenue South
New York, NY 10016

ISBN 978-1-4547-0788-2

Library of Congress Cataloging-in-Publication Data

1,000 beads / introduction by Kristina Logan.
        pages cm

    ISBN 978-1-4547-0788-2 (pbk.)
  1. Beads. 2. Beadwork. I. Logan, Kristina (Artist) II. Lark Crafts (Firm) III. Title: One thousand beads. IV. Title: 1000 beads.
    TT860.A185 2014
    745.58'2--dc23

                                2013032420

Distributed in Canada by Sterling Publishing
c/o Canadian Manda Group, 165 Dufferin Street
Toronto, Ontario, Canada M6K 3H6
Distributed in the United Kingdom by GMC Distribution Services
Castle Place, 166 High Street, Lewes, East Sussex, England BN7 1XU
Distributed in Australia by Capricorn Link (Australia) Pty. Ltd.
P.O. Box 704, Windsor, NSW 2756, Australia

For information about custom editions, special sales, and premium and corporate purchases, please contact Sterling Special Sales at 800-805-5489 or specialsales@sterlingpublishing.com.

Email academic@larkbooks.com for information about desk and examination copies.
The complete policy can be found at larkcrafts.com.
Every effort has been made to ensure that all the information in this book is accurate. However, due to differing conditions, tools, and individual skills, the publisher cannot be responsible for any injuries, losses, and other damages that may result from the use of the information in this book.

Manufactured in China

2 4 6 8 10 9 7 5 3 1

larkcrafts.com

contents

introduction

Beads: They have a power that belies their size. They've been around for at least 40,000 years. They've been found on every piece of land occupied by man. Small objects of enormous impact, beads can teach us about past cultures—about religious beliefs, social systems, and aesthetic trends—or be taken at face value and simply enjoyed as works of art.

Without a doubt, beads have occupied a consistent and enduring place in human history. Archeologists have uncovered them in gravesites, where they were carefully stored, implying that the deceased wanted to carry

them into the afterlife. Beads have been carved on ancient statues and rendered in prominent paintings. Throughout the ages, they've served as currency and as symbols of religious belief. And, of course, they've been used for straightforward adornment in jewelry and clothing.

While beads have undeniable historical relevance, their influence is also very personal. The hole in a bead is there for stringing and suggests a direct connection to the human body—to the neck, wrist, ankle, or ear.

These tiny objects have been an important part of my own life for more than 20 years. I took up beadmaking at a time when I was carving large figurative sculptures out of wood. I wanted to embellish the figures, so I created beads for them. And then I created more. As it turns out, I never put the beads on my sculptures, because I'd become completely captivated by them.

Over time, my interest in the history and making of beads evolved into a career. Today I make beads out of glass and teach beadmaking workshops across the globe. I've spoken to bead collectors and scholars from around

JED GREEN
Brooch ■ 2012

the world. Together, we've speculated about how ancient cultures created the holes in their beads and about why they used specific colors and patterns. I've run my fingers through vast collections of new and ancient beads and wondered about the previous hands that held them. Where did they come from—or travel to?

When I received a phone call from Lark asking me to serve as juror for *1000 Beads*, I felt honored. As I thought about the book, a flash of excitement came over me and many fascinating questions came to mind. What would the pieces submitted for the book look like? What motivates today's artists to create such tiny, intimate objects? Are those artists trying to tell us something, communicate a specific message?

As juror, my goal was to assemble a broad selection of work—one that

BRONWEN HEILMAN
The Flowers of Rudston ■ 2013

1000
beads

JANIE TRAINOR
Three Colorful Etched Beads with Spirals ■ 2012

included beaded jewelry, beaded beads, and individual beads. The entries I reviewed—nearly 3,000, all told—were outstanding, and narrowing them down was a challenge. As you'll see when you flip through these pages, the beads in this collection are made of many different materials: glass, metal, polymer clay, paper, wood, plastic, and rubber. Some of them are so ornate that they can stand on their own as tiny sculptures. Others are more conservative, marked by a simplicity that suggests they be strung in multitudes. Each one calls out to the viewer in its own unique way.

Fragile or durable, precious or cheap, materials are just one of many aspects to consider when viewing the beads in this book. During the jurying process, I was amazed by the diversity of styles and techniques used by the artists. Bronwen Heilman's breathtaking piece *The Flowers of Rudston* features

a technique the artist created herself—a procedure that makes it possible for her to enamel artwork onto a flameworked glass bead. Jed Green used delicate ceramic-transfer patterns to make his dainty *Brooch*. The edgy, colorful *PB2* by Lucy Liu is composed of tube-riveted paper and metal. And Janie Trainor's whimsical, stringer-drawn embellishments make *Three Colorful Etched Beads with Spirals* a standout.

The bead is an ancient form, but—as the innovative pieces in this

collection prove—one that has the power to inspire contemporary artists. The beads being made today are artifacts that connect us and thread us to the past. I would've included many more of them in this book had there been space. I hope that the work you see here inspires you to collect and perhaps create your own beads. Above all, I hope you gain an appreciation for these simple objects that have the potential to tell us so much about ourselves.

—Kristina Logan

LILY LIU
PB2 ■ 2013

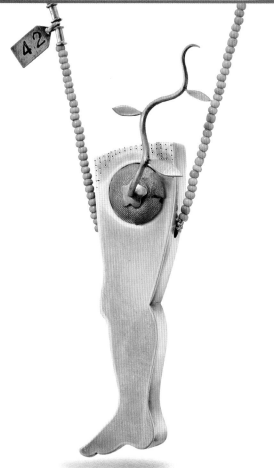
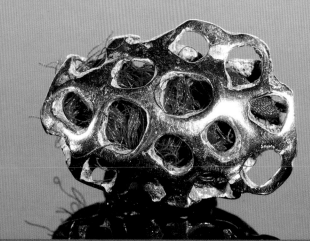

the beads

BARBARA SIMON
Quote Beads ■ 2012

Largest bead: 3 x 3 x 3 cm
Soft glass, colored pencils, gilder's
paste, oil paint; sgrafitto, annealed
PHOTOGRAPHY BY BABETTE BELMONDO

PEELI ROHINI
Royal Collection ▬ 2013

Dimensions vary
Polymer clay, 24-karat edible-grade gold
leaf, contemporary and vintage Swarovski
crystal rhinestones; appliquéd
PHOTOGRAPHY BY ARTIST

DAYLE DOROSHOW
Spiral Rattle Beads ■ 2011

Each: 2.5 x 1 x 1 cm
Polymer clay, metallic powders, faux ivory; carved
PHOTOGRAPHY BY ARTIST

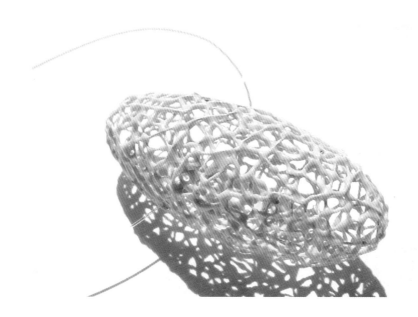

LYNNE GLAZZARD
Aqua Spiral Enameled bead ■ 2012
3.6 x 3.6 x 1.8 cm
Enamel, silver precious metal clay, glass; lampworked, fired
PHOTOGRAPHY BY ARTIST

SIMONE WINKLER
Mint Cocoon #2 ■ 2010
3.8 x 1.6 x 1.6 cm
Sterling silver, enamel, nylon; wire woven
PHOTOGRAPHY BY ARTIST

JENNIFER PARK
Eye Wood ■ 2013

Each: 1 x 3 x 1 cm
Wooden bead, gold leaf, wood
stain; wood-burning techniques
PHOTOGRAPHY BY ARTIST

PATTY LAKINSMITH
Marbled Series ■ 2010

Left: 3.8 x 2.5 cm; center: 4.5 x 2 cm; right: 5 x 2.7 cm
Soda-lime glass; flameworked using gravity technique
PHOTOGRAPHY BY DAVID ORR

JANICE PEACOCK
Buddha ■ 2011
6 x 3.5 x 2.5 cm
Soda-lime glass, reduction powder; flameworked
PHOTOGRAPHY BY AZAD

WIWAT KAMOLPORNWIJIT
Lantern Festival ■ 2011

5 x 50 x 3.7 cm
Polymer clay; hand formed, layered, sliced
PHOTOGRAPHY BY ARTIST

VERA RÖDER
Geometric ■ 2011

Each: 5.1 x 1.2 x 1.2 cm
Soda-lime glass; flameworked,
sandblasted, painted, fused
PHOTOGRAPHY BY ARTIST

AMANDA SCHLEEDE
Caged Dreams ■ 2012

Each: 1.9 x 1.9 x 1.9 cm
Glass, silver precious metal clay; flameworked
PHOTOGRAPHY BY ARTIST

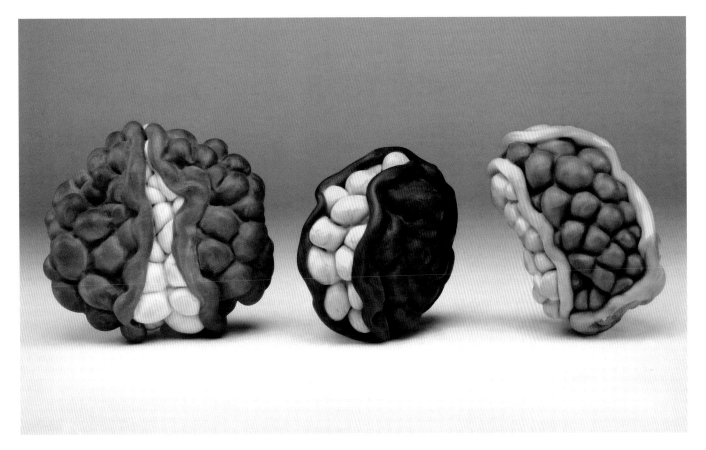

AMY LEMAIRE
Ripe Bead Group ■ 2013

Dimensions vary
Soda-lime glass; flameworked, cold worked
PHOTOGRAPHY BY ARTIST

PETER HOOGEBOOM
From the Year of the Ox Series:
Noodle Necklace ■ 2010
38 x 21 x 1 cm
Porcelain, Bakelite, nylon; beaded
PHOTOGRAPHY BY FRANCIS WILLEMSTIJN

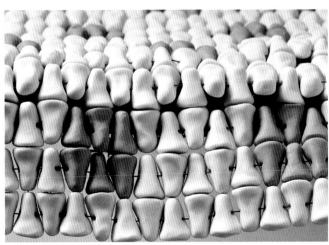

BLAKE WILLIAMS
From the Handmade/Homemade
Series: Nourish ■ 2010

90 x 47.5 x 37.5 cm
Porcelain, wire, antique kitchen chair; hand built
PHOTOGRAPHY BY TIM THAYER

21

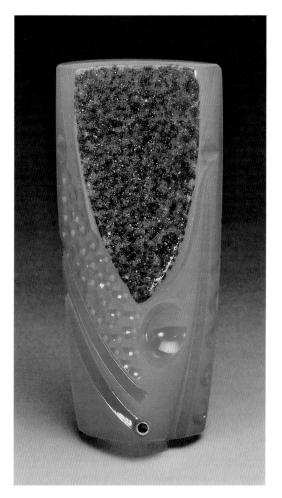

LEIGH ROSS
Flower Garden ■ 2013
5 x 3.5 x 1 cm
Polymer clay, sterling silver; cane work
PHOTOGRAPHY BY STEPHEN ROSS

TOM FINNERAN
Dragonfly Transformation Mask ■ 2012
5.8 x 2.6 x 1.2 cm
Brazilian drusy agate, sterling silver
tube; lapidary techniques
PHOTOGRAPHY BY DAVE BURCHETT

JOO HYUNG PARK
Cut ■ 2010
25 x 5 x 5 cm
Brass, string; soldered, cut, tied
PHOTOGRAPHY BY ARTIST

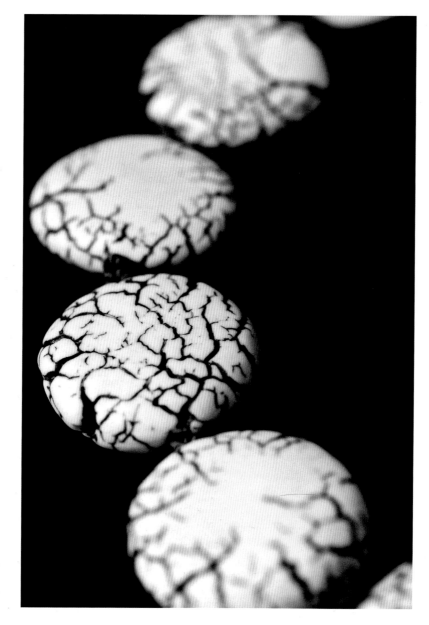

NIINA MAHLBERG
Les Galets ■ 2012
Each bead: 2 x 2 x 0.3 cm
Ceramic; fabricated
PHOTOGRAPHY BY ARTIST

JOANNA PETERS
Pacific Memories ■ 2013
5 x 1.3 x 1.1 cm
Seal tooth, ebony, silk string; carved, inlaid
PHOTOGRAPHY BY ARTIST

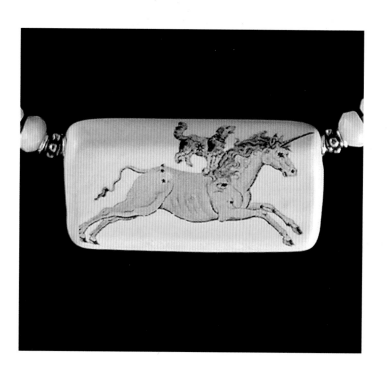

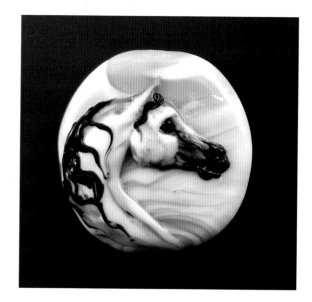

COURTNEY DICARLO
MARY ENGEL
Unicorn with Pup ■ 2011
2 x 4.5 x 0.8 cm
Ceramic with decal; handmade, glazed
PHOTOGRAPHY BY ARTISTS

KERRI FUHR
Arabian ■ 2011
1.5 x 1.5 x 0.2 cm
Glass; lampworked
PHOTOGRAPHY BY ARTIST

VANESSA BACKER
Brown Dog ■ 2012
7.5 x 6 x 2.2 cm
Hand-sculpted porcelain clay, underglazes; fired, cone 02
PHOTOGRAPHY BY STEVE ROSSMAN

1000
beads

ALI VANDEGRIFT
Sandstone and Tuxedo Bicone ■ 2012

12.3 x 3.4 x 3.4 cm
Sandstone glass; lampworked,
capped, decorated
PHOTOGRAPHY BY ARTIST

MINORI TAKAGI
Swirl ■ 2012

Each bead: 2 x 2.2 x 2 cm
Soft glass; lampworked, etched
PHOTOGRAPHY BY SUZANNE GOODWIN

LAURIE NESSEL
Gila Monster ■ 2012
3.6 x 3.6 x 3.6 cm
Soda-lime glass; flameworked

TAMARA GRÜNER
Zeit, die Verwelkt ■ 2012
6.8 x 2.3 x 2.3 cm
Porcelain; cast

BARBARA FAJARDO
White on Black Desert Design ■ 2013

Left: 5.1 x 3.2 x 0.3 cm
Two beads on right: 5.7 x 1.3 x 0.6 cm
Polymer clay, wood tiles; sculpted, carved
PHOTOGRAPHY BY ARTIST

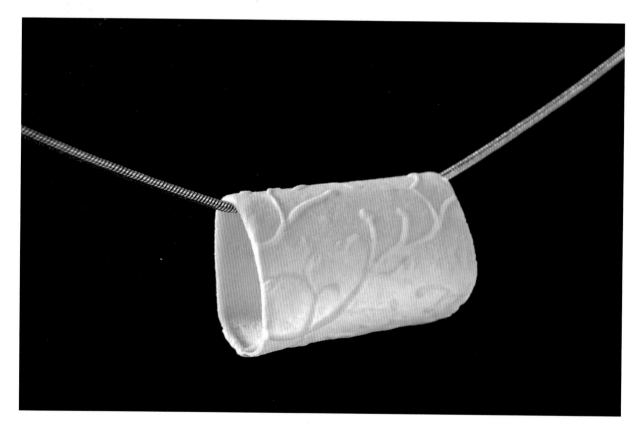

CYNTHIA GAVIÃO
Triangle ■ 2013
1.5 x 2 x 1.5 cm
Porcelain, paper clay; fired, cone 9
PHOTOGRAPHY BY PAULO SILVA

BONNIE LAMBERT
Gourd ■ 2012

Focal bead: 6.5 x 6.5 x 6.5 cm
Wild gourd; drilled, hollowed
PHOTOGRAPHY BY TOM FERRIS

33

ANDREW WELCH
Pebble Beads ■ 2013
Each: 2.2 x 3.5 x 2.9 cm
Polyurethane resin; cast
PHOTOGRAPHY BY ARTIST

DANUTA TYDOR
VLODEK TYDOR
Green Porcelain Bead ■ 2012

0.7 x 3.8 x 4.8 cm
Hand-built porcelain; carved, glazed, fired, cone 6
PHOTOGRAPHY BY ARTISTS

LISA PETERS RUSS
The Orange Lantern ■ 2013

1.2 x 3.4 x 1.2 cm
Stoneware, overglaze; fired, cone 6
PHOTOGRAPHY BY ARTIST

IRIS MISHLY
Brocade Collection Beads ■ 2013

Each bead: 5 x 5 x 2 cm
Polymer clay, powders; textured
PHOTOGRAPHY BY ARTIST

HAROLD COONEY
Nevada Trade Beads ▪ 2013

Dimensions vary
Glass; lampworked, lapidary techniques
PHOTOGRAPHY BY KONNIE SMART

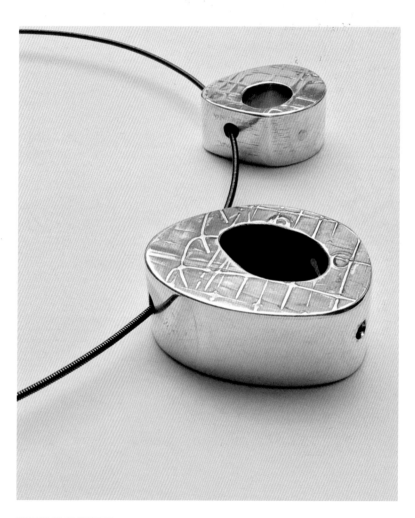

ANNE RANDALL
Bunny Foo Foo ■ 2013
1.5 x 0.8 x 0.3 cm
Sterling silver, resin; hand formed
PHOTOGRAPHY BY ARTIST

MICHAEL BANNER
MAUREEN BANNER
Big Fat Bead ■ 2013
2.5 x 2.2 x 0.7 cm
Sterling silver; hollow formed, textured
PHOTOGRAPHY BY MAUREEN BANNER

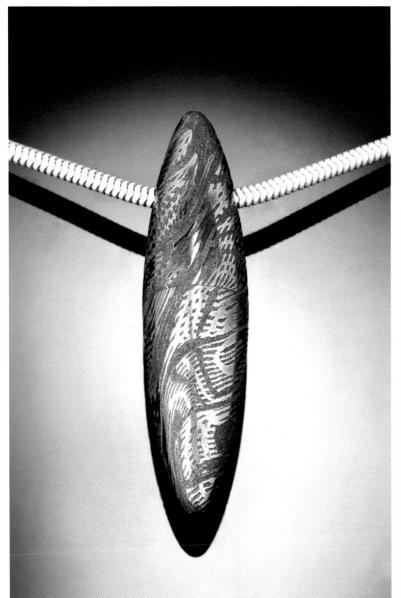

JASON MORRISSEY
Damascus Urn Bead for Raina Davis Jensen ■ 2013
5 x 1.7 cm
Tool steel composite billet Damascus
PHOTOGRAPHY BY DEREK MASTEN

RUBY PILVEN
Handmade Porcelain Candy Pieces ▪ 2013
30 x 30 x 1 cm
Handmade porcelain, hemp cord
PHOTOGRAPHY BY ARTIST

KATHARINA EDER
Fadenspiel Cup Necklace ■ 2012

51 x 3 x 12 cm
Antique bohemian seed beads, thread; crotchet technique
PHOTOGRAPHY BY SIMONE ANDRESS

CYNDI LAVIN
Not Found in Nature, Bead 2 ■ 2013

3.5 x 7 x 4 cm
Found copper plumbing fixture, glass seed beads;
St. Petersburg chain stitch, bead embroidery
PHOTOGRAPHY BY ARTIST

1000
beads

ELEANOR LUX
Planet Beads ■ 2013

2 x 2 x 2 cm
Bugle beads, seed beads; peyote and fringe stitches
PHOTOGRAPHY BY RICHARD QUICK

ANA GOMEZ
Dominoes ■ 2010
48 x 36 x 36 cm
Handmade ceramic beads, dress
PHOTOGRAPHY BY DIEGO PÉREZ

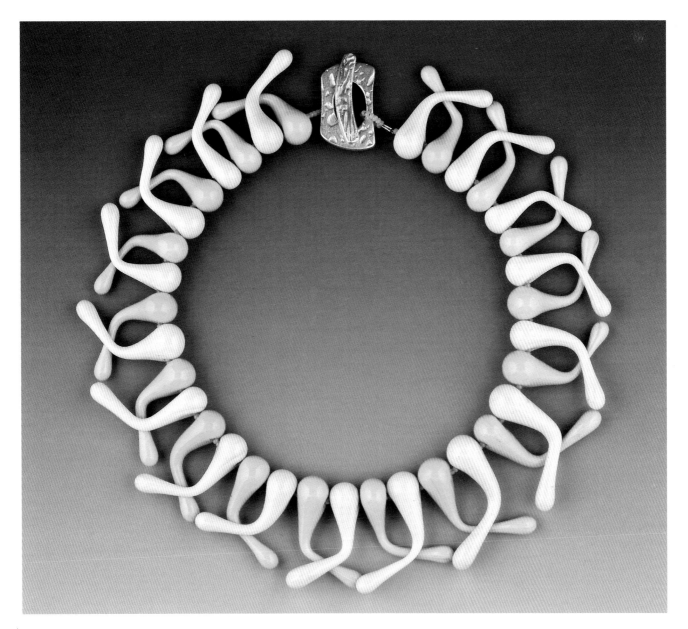

DARLENE DURRWACHTER RUSHING
From the Drip Series: Celadon ■ 2011

16 x 10 x 0.5 cm
Glass, fine silver, seed beads; flameworked
PHOTOGRAPHY BY LARRY BERMAN

TAMARA GRÜNER
Metopa ■ 2012
6 x 2 x 2 cm
Porcelain, plastic; cast, mounted
PHOTOGRAPHY BY ARTIST

ELENA MIKLUSH
Warm Zig-Zag ■ 2013
3.5 x 3 x 3 cm
Nylon thread; micro-macramé
PHOTOGRAPHY BY ARTIST

1000
beads

BIRGIT KUPKE-PEYLA
Smithsonian Pink ■ 2010

17.8 x 17.8 x 2.5 cm
22-karat gold, 14-karat gold, sterling silver, patina,
pink tourmaline; sgraffito, hollow formed, soldered
PHOTOGRAPHY BY ARTIST

47

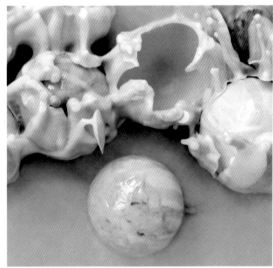

ABIGAIL YOUDIM
Scrumptious ■ 2011
7 x 55 x 45 cm
Polymer and silicon; cast
PHOTOGRAPHY BY EMILY NHAISSI

INGEBORG VANDAMME
Paper Necklace ■ 2013

22 x 22 x 0.6 cm
Paper, silver, silk
PHOTOGRAPHY BY ARTIST

MARGARET ZINSER
Moths ■ 2012

Each: 10 x 6 x 1 cm
Soda-lime glass, vitreous enamels;
flameworked, hand painted
PHOTOGRAPHY BY ARTIST

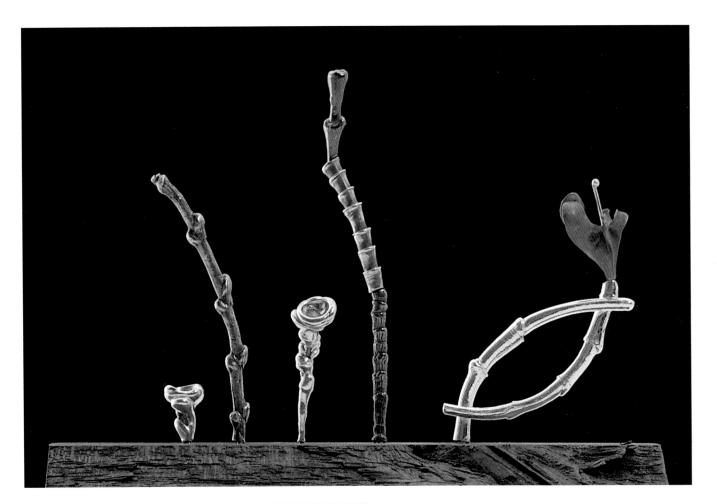

SUSAN ELLENTON
Extruded Buds and Sleeves ■ 2012

Largest bead: 5 x 0.4 x 0.3 cm
Fine silver and copper metal clays, fine
silver tubing; manipulated extrusion
PHOTOGRAPHY BY ARTIST

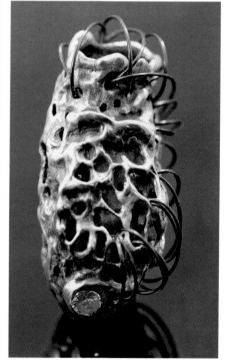

MARJORIE RENNO
Papoose Basket ■ 2012
1.5 x 0.8 x 0.5 cm
Wild cucumber pod, precious metal clay,
cubic zirconia, copper wire; woven
PHOTOGRAPHY BY MIKE LECLAIR

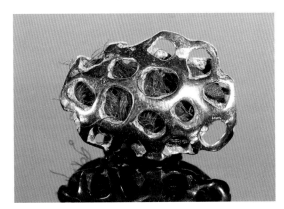

CHIHIRO MAKIO
Flora Necklace ■ 2010

1.2 x 20 x 1.2 0 cm
Sterling silver; oxidized, rhodium plated, hand
crafted, soldered, assembled, connected
PHOTOGRAPHY BY MOBILIA GALLERY

SHAUNA BURKE
You're Not So Tough ■ 2012

2.5 x 4 x 1.7 cm
Sterling silver, enamel, wool thread; oxidized,
fabricated, formed, soldered, embellished
PHOTOGRAPHY BY NAOMI WHITE

INGEBORG VANDAMME
Landscape ■ 2013
10 x 10 x 2.5 cm
Paper, silver; soldered
PHOTOGRAPHY BY ARTIST

MARINA MONICA MEDINA
Volverte a Ver ■ 2013

Each: 4 x 2 x 2 cm
Silk cocoons, natural silk thread,
bronze wire, ink; caligraphy
PHOTOGRAPHY BY ARTIST

FABIENNE SCHALLER
Stripes ■ 2012

Largest bead: 3 x 3 x 3 cm
Merino wool, metal chain; wet felted, hand
shaped, embroidered, embellished
PHOTOGRAPHY BY MARY KNIGHT AND ARTIST

MARY LOU TOMPKINS
Mother Feline ■ 2012
2.3 x 1.8 x 1 cm
Stoneware clay, glaze, paint; hand
carved, electric fired, cone 5/6
PHOTOGRAPHY BY GLENN HUDSON

MARCY LAMBERSON
Sprocket ■ 2013
5.7 x 1.3 x 3.2 cm
Soft glass; flameworked
PHOTOGRAPHY BY ANDY ALLEN

DEBRA RYMAN
Black Irid Swirly ■ 2012
2.5 x 2.5 x 2.5 cm
Soda-lime glass; flameworked,
stringer application
PHOTOGRAPHY BY ARTIST

DOLORES BARRETT
Cobalt Precious Bead ■ 2012
1 x 1 cm
Glass, 24-karat gold foil;
fused, slumped, drilled
PHOTOGRAPHY BY ARTIST

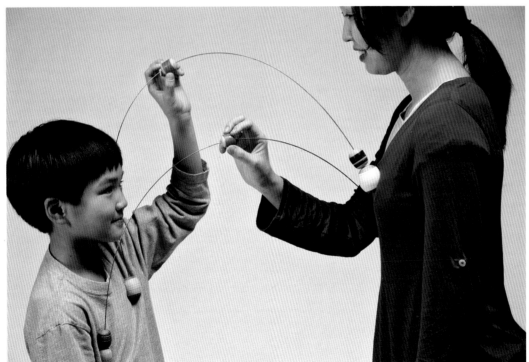

SUNYOUNG CHEONG
Beads Maze ■ 2012

Dimensions vary
Construction paper, wood, aluminum tube, rare earth
magnet, wire, glue; lathe turned, hand fabricated
PHOTOGRAPHY BY AARON PADEN

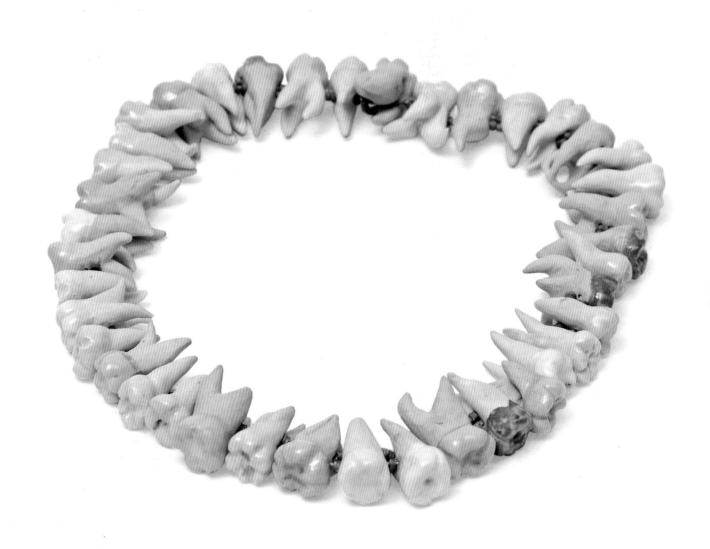

MARION DELARUE
Trophy Jewel ■ 2010
20 x 19 x 21 cm
Stoneware, porcelain;
hand modeled, glazed
PHOTOGRAPHY BY ARTIST

1000
beads

KAREN MASSARO
Necklace 4 ■ 2012
0.6 x 60 x 3.5 cm
Porcelain, glaze, onyx; slip cast
PHOTOGRAPHY BY PAUL SCRAUB

GALIT EINAV
Imagination ■ 2013
9 x 8.5 x 4 cm
Linen thread, wire
PHOTOGRAPHY BY AMOS TRABOLSKY

1000
beads

NOFAR BUYUM
A Bead, a Hasp, a Pendant ■ 2013

3 x 5 x 3 cm
Leather, copper, enamel
PHOTOGRAPHY BY ARTIST

NIINA MAHLBERG
One Day News ■ 2012
Each bead: 3.5 x 4 x 0.2 cm
Ceramic, newspaper; cast
PHOTOGRAPHY BY ARTIST

LOUISE LITTLE
Arizona Rock Art ■ 2012
3.2 x 5.7 x 5.7 cm
Soda-lime glass, brass, bronze and silver bead caps;
hollow blown, lampworked, tube riveted, etched, painted
PHOTOGRAPHY BY ARTIST

DORIS HÄUSLER
Paper Beads ■ 2013
Largest bead: 3.3 x 2 cm
Book pages, acrylic; laminated
PHOTOGRAPHY BY ARTIST

KIMBERLY HUESTIS
Porcelain Pebble Bead Necklace ■ 2013

Each bead: 1.6 x 1.6 x 1.5 cm
Porcelain clay; hand shaped
PHOTOGRAPHY BY TINYSTUDIO.COM

MIRIAM PAPPALARDO
Pong Necklace ■ 2010
36 x 28 x 4 cm
Ping-pong balls, plastic, rubber
band; compressed, drilled
PHOTOGRAPHY BY ARNALDO PAPPALARDO

SABINE LITTLE
Moongazing Hare ■ 2013
6 x 3.3 x 2.5 cm
Soda-lime glass, steel wire; flameworked
PHOTOGRAPHY BY ARTIST

LIZ LOTT
Foo Foo ■ 2011
2.8 x 1.8 x 1.1 cm
Porcelain, underglaze; hand sculpted and painted
PHOTOGRAPHY BY ARTIST

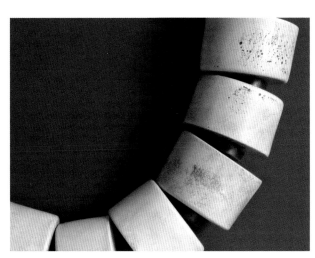

CHECHA SOKOLOVIC
Untitled ▨ 2012

Each bead: 2 x 3 x 3 cm
Cement; cast, hand polished
PHOTOGRAPHY BY BARBARA COHEN

69

JU-HYUN LEE
Mal-Lang Mal-Lang ■ 2013
28 x 28 x 6 cm
Silicone; mixed media
PHOTOGRAPHY BY ARTIST

FLORIANE LATAILLE
Tricot Noir and Blanc Pendant ■ 2012

6 x 6 x 6 cm
Soft glass, silver; flameworked
PHOTOGRAPHY BY ARTIST

JED GREEN
Necklace 1 ■ 2012
60 x 10 x 5 cm
Borosilicate glass, silver, paint, ceramic
transfer, rock crystal; flameworked
PHOTOGRAPHY BY RUSSELL SADUR

73

KATE ROTHRA FLEMING
Urchin Bead ■ 2012

1 x 1.3 x 1 cm
Soda-lime glass, dichroic
glass; flameworked
PHOTOGRAPHY BY RICK RHODES

SANDRA BORNEMANN
Blue Disc ■ 2012
2 x 3.3 x 2 cm
Soda-lime glass, enamel, silver
bead caps; flameworked
PHOTOGRAPHY BY DIETER BORNEMANN

VALÉRIE VAYRE
Untitled ■ 2011
3 x 3 x 1.5 cm
Glass, silver leaf; flameworked
PHOTOGRAPHY BY ARTIST

JOELLE SHAFTER
Electrifying ■ 2013

1.5 x 5.5 x 9 cm
Satin ribbon, felt, freshwater pearls, wire;
hand dyed, rolled, beaded, crocheted
PHOTOGRAPHY BY ALEXANDRA SHAFTER

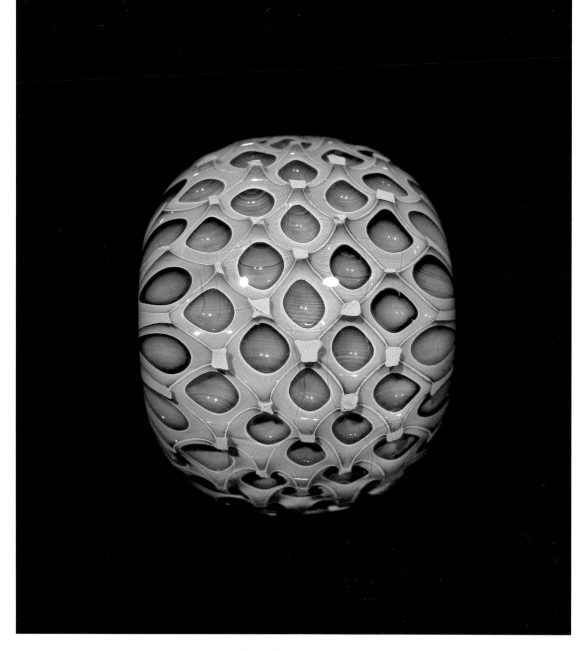

TRAVIS WEBER
Sterling ■ 2011
2.8 x 2.3 x 2.8 cm
Borosilicate glass; flameworked
PHOTOGRAPHY BY ARTIST

IVONNE PALACIOS
Pebbles ■ 2013
6.3 x 3.9 x 3.8 cm
Merino wool, silk; wet felted
PHOTOGRAPHY BY ARTIST

SZILVIA VIHRIÄLÄ
Harlequin Bunny Bead ■ 2013
3.1 x 2 x 2 cm
Hand-formed white earthenware, clear glaze; electric
fired, cone 09, refired in sauna stove, cone 06
PHOTOGRAPHY BY ARTIST

CHARLENE MODENA
Endangered ■ 2012
25 x 38 x 19 cm
Copper, sterling silver, enamel; cast
PHOTOGRAPHY BY D.J. FELTON

ELISE STRAUSS
Trumpeter Swan Pair ■ 2012
Largest swan: 4.4 cm wide
Soda-lime glass; lampworked, etched
PHOTOGRAPHY BY ARTIST

JULIE LONG GALLEGOS
Pearl Baubles ■ 2012

Largest bead: 2.5 cm in diameter
Freshwater natural seed pearls, wooden forms,
sterling silver chain; hand oxidized, beadweaving

PHOTOGRAPHY BY GEORGE POST

JESSICA ARMSTRONG
Growth ■ 2013
3.8 x 4.4 x 5.8 cm
Microbeads, resin, sterling silver, cubic zirconium
PHOTOGRAPHY BY ERIN CORA TURNER

KATHERINE WADSWORTH
Cherry Tree in Bloom ■ 2012
4.8 x 1.2 cm
Glass; lampworked, acid etched
PHOTOGRAPHY BY BRAD MOON

LEE SCHEIN
Purple Fibers ■ 2013
5 x 2.5 x 3 cm
Merino wool, thread, gold fiber, clay beads;
handmade, painted, felted, embroidered
PHOTOGRAPHY BY ARTIST

ALISA LETCIUS
Sticks Beads ■ 2011
Each bead: 5 x 1 x 1 cm
Polymer clay; hand shaped, baked
PHOTOGRAPHY BY ARTIST

FABIENNE SCHALLER
Mexican Garden ■ 2012

Dimensions vary
Merino wool, glass beads; wet felted, hand
shaped, embroidered, embellished
PHOTOGRAPHY BY MARY KNIGHT AND ARTIST

KERIE TONKIN
Loaf ■ 2013
30 x 20 cm
Sterling silver, cotton; hand pierced, stamped
PHOTOGRAPHY BY CRAIG TONKIN

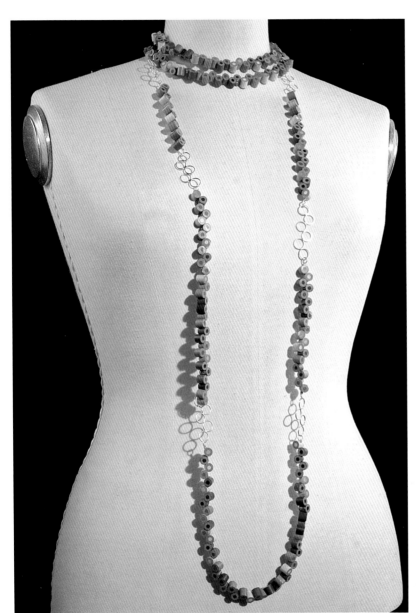

MARIA OCHOA
Untitled ■ 2010

66 x 15 x 1 cm
Sterling silver, colored pencils, stainless steel
wire, beading thread; fabricated, hammered
PHOTOGRAPHY BY SPIROS

85

CRISTINA ZANI
My Seoul Red and Gold Necklace ■ 2013
28 x 9 x 3 cm
24-karat gold-plated brass, wood, acrylic paint, 24-karat
gold leaf, linen thread; sanded, burned, threaded
PHOTOGRAPHY BY ARTIST

1000
beads

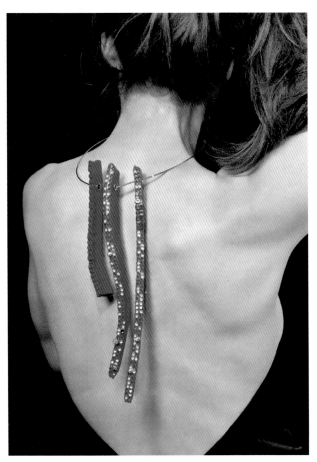

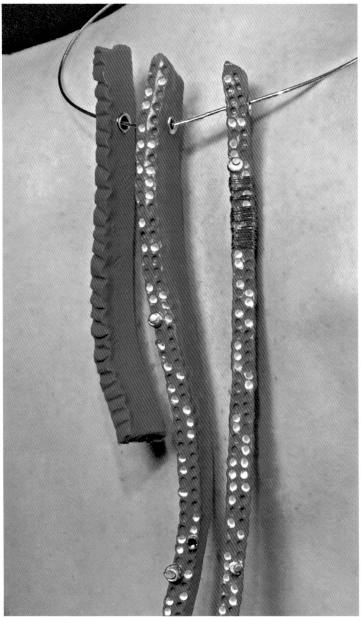

ERIKA FERRARIN
From the Heavy Is Beautiful Series: Octo: Pie ■ 2011
29 x 7.6 x 1.9 cm
Earthenware clay, ceramic paint, metal end caps, Swarovski
crystal; electric fired, hand formed, textured, and painted
PHOTOGRAPHY BY LEN WARD

SHELBY FITZPATRICK
Stripes ■ 2012
20 x 20 x 2 cm
Silver, wood, mokume gane, copper beads;
fused, fabricated, married metal
PHOTOGRAPHY BY MIKE BLISSETT

RICK WOLTER
Exotic Wood Beads with Sterling Silver Caps ■ 2013
Left: 6.7 x 1.6 cm; right: 4.6 x 2.2 cm
Burmese rosewood, ebony, sterling silver;
cored on drill press, lathed, polished
STERLING SILVER WORK BY TAMMY WOLTER
PHOTOGRAPHY BY DAVID ORR

RIA LINS
Emptiness and Strength ■ 2010
30 x 3 x 1 cm
Flax clay and cord; smoked
PHOTOGRAPHY BY DRIES VAN DEN BRANDE

CHRISTINE DAVIES
Orbital with Garnets ■ 2012
Large bead: 3.5 x 3.5 x 3.5 cm
Silver, garnets; gold plated,
rapid prototyped, cast
PHOTOGRAPHY BY ARTIST

ISABELLE POSILLICO
Time Ribbon Bead ■ 2012

1.3 x 1.3 x 1.3 cm
Sterling silver, 18-karat gold, diamonds;
rollerprinted, constructed, soldered, oxidized

LISA ATCHISON
Emergence ■ 2012
5.6 x 2.5 x 2.5 cm
Soda-lime glass, silver, cubic zirconias; flameworked
PHOTOGRAPHY BY ARTIST

MINORI TAKAGI
Cherry Blossoms ■ 2012
3 x 2.5 x 1 cm
Soft glass, mica; lampworked
PHOTOGRAPHY BY SUZANNE GOODWIN

ERIKA FERRARIN
From the Tentacles Series: Viola Tentacles ■ 2012

11.5 x 9.5 x 3.8 cm
Earthenware clay, rubber tubing, silver findings, bone; hand
textured, electric fired, glazed, strung, knotted, hand formed
PHOTOGRAPHY BY LEN WARD

93

KIMBERLY ROGERS
Lampwonk Studnik ■ 2012
1.5 x 2.8 x 1.3 cm
Soda-lime glass, baking soda,
steel nails; flameworked
PHOTOGRAPHY BY ARTIST

BONNIE POLINSKI
Banded Tree ■ 2013
3.1 x 2.8 x 1.3 cm
Clay, glaze, fine silver, sterling silver, brass; raku
fired, soldered, silversmithing techniques
PHOTOGRAPHY BY ARTIST

DOLORES BARRETT
Purple Geode Bead ■ 2011

2 x 1 x 1 cm
Glass and dichroic frit; fused, slumped, carved
PHOTOGRAPHY BY ARTIST

KAY BONITZ
Bead with Pearls ■ 2013

2.5 x 1.5 x 0.5 cm
Polymer clay, pearls; die formed,
silk-screened, image transfer
PHOTOGRAPHY BY WERNER BONITZ

95

BONNIE LAMBERT
Paper ■ 2012

Dimensions vary
Paper, thread; sewn
PHOTOGRAPHY BY TOM FERRIS

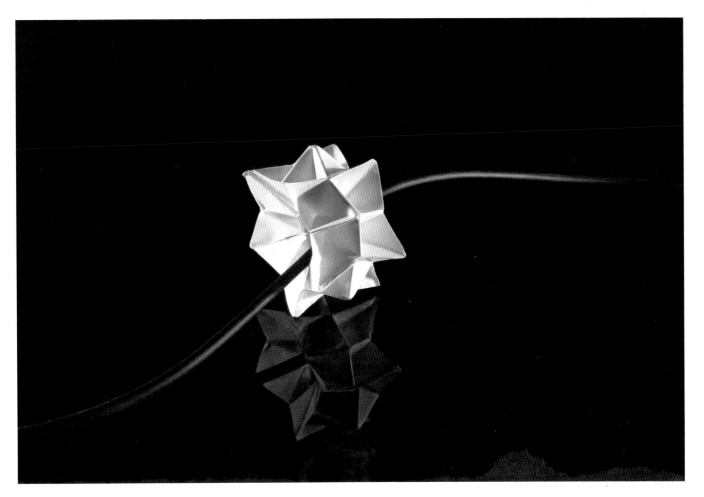

GEORGIA GREMOUTI
Modules 1 ▦ 2013

3 x 3 x 3 cm
Paper; folded
PHOTOGRAPHY BY ARTIST

LILIANA CIRSTEA GLENN
Female Effigy: Shamanka ■ 2013

80.3 x 60.8 x 60.6 cm
Soda-lime glass, brass, hemp, brass tube; flameworked,
etched, braided, acid etched, darkened, metalwork
PHOTOGRAPHY BY ARTIST

RUBY PILVEN
Handmade Porcelain Beads ■ 2013
30 x 30 x 1 cm
Handmade porcelain, decals, glaze
PHOTOGRAPHY BY ARTIST

ANNE LONDEZ
Red Splash ■ 2011
5 x 4 x 4 cm
Soda-lime glass, cubic zirconium; blown, flameworked
PHOTOGRAPHY BY ARTIST

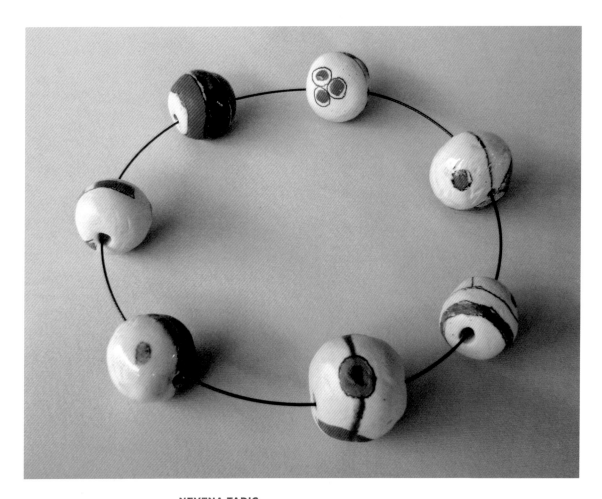

NEVENA TADIC
Red, Blue, and White Porcelain Beads ■ 2011

Necklace: 16 cm in diameter; each bead: 3 cm
Porcelain, underglazes, glaze; hand rolled, fired, cone 6
PHOTOGRAPHY BY ARTIST

STEPHANIE GOUGH
Damask ■ 2013
Each bead: 1.4 x 1.5 x 0.8 cm
Soda-lime glass, enamel; flameworked, sandblasted
PHOTOGRAPHY BY ARTIST

NANCY CAIN
Slider Beads ■ 2008
Each: 2 x 2 x 2 cm
Japanese seed beads, Swarovski crystal
bicones; off-loom peyote stitch
PHOTOGRAPHY BY DAVE WOLVERTON

1000
beads

MAYRA NIEVES-BEKELE
Glass Skirt ■ 2012

Each: 5 x 5 x 5 cm
Seed beads, glass beads, felted
ball; bead embroidery
PHOTOGRAPHY BY GEORGE POST

GAIL FINNEY
Graffiti Bead ■ 2012
2 x 1.3 x 0.5 cm
Soda-lime glass, ceramic pencil
sketch; flameworked

ANNE LONDEZ
Coral Vessel Bead ■ 2011
4.5 x 4 x 4 cm
Soda-lime glass, silver foil; flameworked

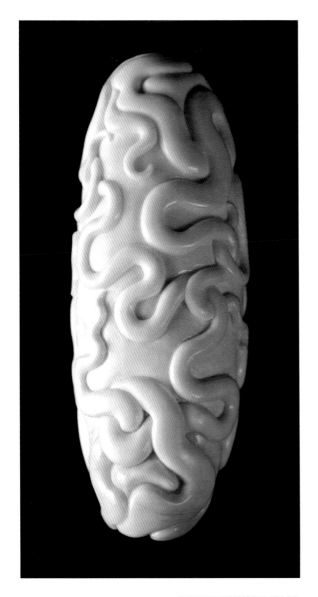

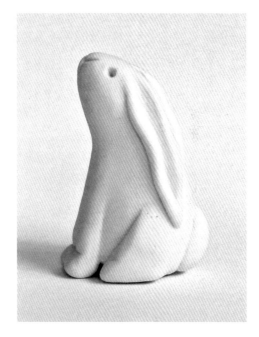

HANNE ERIKSEN MAPP
Untitled ■ 2013
11.5 x 4.4 x 4.4 cm
Sperm whale ivory; hand engraved
PHOTOGRAPHY BY ARTIST

CAROLINE DEWISON
Moongazing Hare ■ 2013
4.7 x 3 x 2.4 cm
Sculpted porcelain
PHOTOGRAPHY BY ARTIST

MIRIAM STEGER-VAN DER SCHRIECK
Shocking Pink ■ 2012

Overall length: 48 cm
Glass; flameworked, encased
PHOTOGRAPHY BY ARTIST

AMBER BALLARD
Rainbow Spikes ■ 2012
3.2 x 0.6 x 0.6 cm
Soft glass; flameworked
PHOTOGRAPHY BY ARTIST

CAROL BLACKBURN
Tetra Beads ■ 2012
Each: 3.2 x 3.2 x 3.2 cm
Polymer clay
PHOTO BY ARTIST

LYDIA MUELL
Vintage ■ 2013
3.3 x 3.3 x 1.3 cm
Glass; stringer application

SALLY (SEUNG HEE) LEE
Ego Trip1-1 ■ 2011
4 x 4 x 2 cm
Borosilicate glass, sterling silver, pearls,
coral, fishing line; lampworked

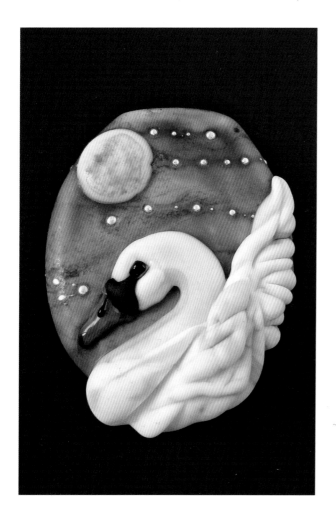

KERRI FUHR
Swan Song ■ 2011
2 x 1.5 x 0.3 cm
Glass, enamel, fine silver; lampworked, etched

JODIE MCDOUGALL
Mayan Bird ■ 2013
1.5 x 1.3 x 0.5 cm
Glass; flameworked, murrini

JOSEAN GARCIA
Loopy ■ 2013
Overall length: 48 cm
Blown glass, black silicone tube; roll-up technique
PHOTOGRAPHY BY ARTIST

LINDA EDEIKEN
Red/Green Beaded Beads ■ 2012
45.7 x 2.5 x 2.5 cm
African beads, various antique beads;
beaded, stitched, sewn
PHOTOGRAPHY BY MELINDA HOLDEN

ANNIE DUNBAR
Rainforest Mosaic ■ 2012
6 x 2 x 2 cm
Polymer clay, metallic ink
PHOTOGRAPHY BY ARTIST

PAULA BEST
Art Girl ■ 2012
3 x 1 x 1 cm
Fabric, beads; embellished, hand stitched
PHOTOGRAPHY BY ARTIST

LORETTA LAM
The Red Pod ■ 2012
53 x 2.8 x 2 cm
Polymer clay, coconut shell, wooden beads, barrel
clasp; hollow formed, millefiori, Skinner blend
PHOTOGRAPHY BY DOUG YAPLE

BEAU BARRETT
Graphene Matrix ■ 2012
7 x 2 x 2 cm
Borosilicate glass, frit; hollow blown
PHOTOGRAPHY BY ARTIST

LESLIE SCHENKEL
Loose Beads ■ 2013
Dimensions vary
Glass; flameworked
PHOTOGRAPHY BY TIM LESTER

L. SUE SZABO
Organic Pod Earrings ■ 2010
. Each: 5 x 2 x 2 cm
Sterling silver; hand fabricated, soldered, forged
PHOTOGRAPHY BY ARTIST

JED GREEN
Brooch ■ 2012
16 x 12 x 2.5 cm
Borosilicate glass, paint, silver, ceramic
transfer; lampworked, etched
PHOTOGRAPHY BY RUSSELL SADUR

LORI FLANDERS
Healing Hearts ■ 2012

Each bead: 5.1 x 2.5 x 1.3 cm
Glass, fine silver; flameworked
PHOTOGRAPHY BY ARTIST

JACK JENNINGS
Lariat ■ 2011

3 x 2 x 2 cm
Sterling silver, 18-karat gold, iolite;
formed, fabricated, oxidized
PHOTOGRAPHY BY ARTIST

KATHERINE WADSWORTH
Red Lady's Slipper Orchid Bead ■ 2010
4.5 x 2 x 1 cm
Glass; lampworked, acid etched
PHOTOGRAPHY BY BRAD MOON

MARILYN PERAZA
White Sculptural Rose ■ 2013
1 x 1.5 x 1.5 cm
Soda-lime glass; flameworked, sculpted, etched
PHOTOGRAPHY BY ARTIST

HAROLD COONEY
District of Columbia Trade Beads ■ 2013

Dimensions vary
Glass; lampworked, lapidary techniques
PHOTOGRAPHY BY KONNIE SMART

KELLY ROBERGE
Mokume Gane Bead Extravaganza ■ 2013

Each bead: 5 x 5 x 1.5 cm
Polymer clay, mokume gane
PHOTOGRAPHY BY GREG SAWYER

ANDREA SYMONS
Celadon in Cedar ■ 2013

3.5 x 3.5 x 1.1 cm
Soda-lime glass, silver glass
PHOTOGRAPHY BY ARTIST

TONI LUTMAN
Encased Implosion ■ 2013

3.7 x 2.5 x 2.5 cm
Soda-lime glass; flameworked, encased
PHOTOGRAPHY BY ARTIST

KIM EDWARDS
Glass Dodecahedron Bead ■ 2013
3.3 x 3.3 x 3.3 cm
Borosilicate glass; flameworked, annealed,
chainmaille dodecahedron pattern
PHOTOGRAPHY BY JERRY ANTHONY

BETTY STEPHAN
Jewel ■ 2013
2.5 x 2.5 x 2.5 cm
Seed beads, crystals, felted bead; bead embroidery
PHOTOGRAPHY BY ARTIST

MICHAEL MANGIAFICO
Stage III Cobalt Bead ▪ 2013

11.5 x 11.5 x 11.5 cm
Soda-lime glass; flameworked,
acid washed, etched
PHOTOGRAPHY BY ARTIST

LISA KLAKULAK
Eyed ■ 2013

17.8 x 17.8 x 1.3 cm
Wool fiber, cotton thread; wet felted, hand stitched,
free-motion machine stitched/embossed
PHOTOGRAPHY BY MARY VOGEL

LINDA MAGI
Stripes Bead ■ 2013
1.3 x 0.8 x 0.8 cm
Cotton, argentium silver; hand crocheted, constructed
PHOTOGRAPHY BY ARTIST

ELENA MIKLUSH
Temari Bead ■ 2013
2 x 2 x 2 cm
Cotton thread, nylon thread, ball;
temari, wrapped, embroidered
PHOTOGRAPHY BY ARTIST

INGEBORG VANDAMME
Traces Necklace ■ 2013

20 x 20 x 0.6 cm
Wax paper, bones, silver, silk
PHOTOGRAPHY BY ARTIST

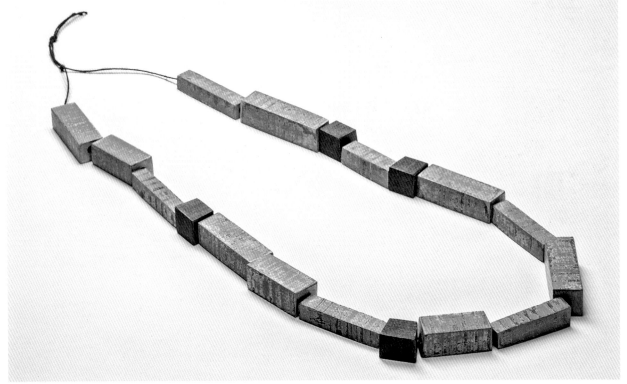

KIMBERLY WINKLE
Block Beads Necklace ■ 2013

Overall length: 20 cm
Poplar, milk paint; hand shaped
PHOTOGRAPHY BY BEN CORDA

MELANIE MOERTEL
Clara ■ 2011
5.8 x 2.5 x 1.1 cm
Glass, 24-karat gold foil; flameworked,
murrini, stringer application
PHOTOGRAPHY BY ARTIST

MANUELA WUTSCHKE
From the Black-and-White Charcoal
Series: Me and the River ■ 2013

6.1 x 2.9 x 1.2 cm
Soda-lime glass, goldstone, enamel;
flameworked, stringer work
PHOTOGRAPHY BY ARTIST

129

ASTRID RIEDEL
Blue Moon ■ 2012
4.2 x 4.2 x 1.3 cm
Glass, enamels; flameworked,
stringer application
PHOTOGRAPHY BY ARTIST

MARTA EDÖCS
Hypnosis ■ 2013
1 x 7 x 1 cm
Soda-lime glass; flameworked,
ground, fire polished
PHOTOGRAPHY BY ESZTER GALAMBOS

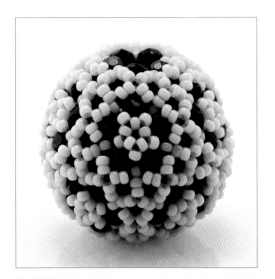

ADRIENNE GASKELL
Spinner Earrings ■ 2012

Each bead: 1.5 x 1 x 0.8 cm
European glass and sterling silver beads, sterling
silver wire; wire work, needle beadweaving

ONYE NDIKA
Doceria (Prototype) ■ 2011

2.2 x 2.2 x 2.2 cm
Czech crystals, seed beads, monofilament;
right-angle weave, triangle weave, netting

KATHRYN DUMMER
Seeds of Strange ▣ 2010

Each bead: 1.5 x 0.8 x 0.8 cm
Polymer clay; cane work

LIBBY MILLS
Ripple Bead Trio ■ 2012
Each bead: 3.8 x 3.8 x 0.5 cm
Polymer clay, aluminum;
ripple-blade cane work
PHOTOGRAPHY BY ARTIST

GAIL FINNEY
Daisy Swirl ■ 2011
2.8 x 0.8 x 0.8 cm
Soda-lime glass, base bead; flameworked, painted
PHOTOGRAPHY BY DAVID ORR

MARIANNE KELLEY
Around the World ■ 2012
2 x 1.3 x 2 cm
Glass; flameworked, engraved, polished
PHOTOGRAPHY BY ANN CADY

ELIZABETH JOHNSON
Glass Gooseberry Beads on Copper Wire Stems ■ 2012

Each bead: 1.5 x 1.5 x 6.5 cm
Soda-lime glass, copper wire; flameworked, acid etched
PHOTOGRAPHY BY ARTIST

GALIT EINAV
Fantasy ■ 2012

Dimensions vary
Enamel beads; knit
PHOTOGRAPHY BY AMOS TRABOLSKY

HOLLY COOPER
Xiufang ■ 2013
4.6 x 2 cm
Glass; flameworked
PHOTOGRAPHY BY ARTIST

ELIZABETH JOHNSON
Glass Strawberry Beads on Copper Wires ■ 2011
Largest bead: 3 x 2.5 x 8.5 cm
Soda-lime glass, copper wire; flameworked, acid etched
PHOTOGRAPHY BY ARTIST

JOHN WINTER
Hidden Island ■ 2012

0.6. x 2.5 x 0.5 cm
Glass, copper leaf, silver leaf, silver wire;
flameworked, threaded stringer, etched

BRONWEN HEILMAN
The Flowers of Rudston ■ 2013

2.3 x 1 x 0.5 cm
Glass, enamel, 22-karat gold; flameworked

DIANA FERGUSON
Scroll Bead Neckpiece—a Riot of Flora ■ 2012

6.5 x 8 x 2.5 cm
Polymer clay, paper scrolls, digital
imagery; hand sculpted and finished
PHOTOGRAPHY BY LARRY SANDERS

139

MAGS BONHAM
Ancient Relics: Three Beauties ■ 2013

3.5 x 1.2 x 1.2 cm
Polymer clay; image transfer, Photoshop
manipulation, carved, antiqued
PHOTOGRAPHY BY ARTIST

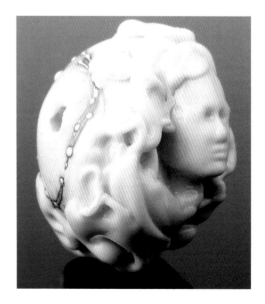

SHIMRIT ZAGORSKY
Urban Tribe ■ 2012
5 x 8 x 5 cm
Plastic beads, metal chains, Swarovski elements, paint
PHOTOGRAPHY BY RAN PLOTNIZKY

SUSAN HOOD
Goddess ■ 2012
3 x 3 x 2 cm
Soda-lime glass, silver wire; flameworked
PHOTOGRAPHY BY MEGAN ELEMENT

KATE ROTHRA FLEMING
Nudibranch Necklace—Flame ■ 2013

1 x 2 x 18 cm
Soda-lime glass, dichroic glass; flameworked,
torch formed, hand fabricated
PHOTOGRAPHY BY FRANK FLEMING

AMY WALDMAN-SMITH
Round Ottoman in Shades of Orange ■ 2012
1.9 x 2.5 x 2.5 cm
Soda-lime glass; lampworked, masked, raked
PHOTOGRAPHY BY ANN CADY

MURIEL DUVAL
Victoria ■ 2011
1.5 x 1 x 1 cm
Soft glass; flameworked
PHOTOGRAPHY BY ARTIST

DANIA CHELMINSKY
DecoStamps Necklace ▪ 2012

Each bead: 3 x 3 x 0.6 cm
Stamps, pearls, stones, epoxy,
silver; hand fabricated, cast
PHOTOGRAPHY BY RAN ERDE

VANESSA BACKER
Three Rabbits ■ 2012

Each: 7 x 3.5 x 2.5 cm
Hand-sculpted porcelain clay, underglazes; fired, cone 02
PHOTOGRAPHY BY STEVE ROSSMAN

SUSAN ELLENTON
Extruded Undulations ■ 2012

Largest bead: 5.6 x 1 x 1 cm
Fine silver, bronze, and copper metal clays, fine silver and copper
tubing, 22-karat gold, Montana sapphire; manipulated extrusion

JILLIAN PALONE
String of Pearls ■ 2011

89 x 22.5 x 10 cm
Paper clay, paint, colored pencils; fabricated, strung
PHOTOGRAPHY BY ARTIST

LORETTA LAM
At the Spice Bazaar ▪ 2011
53 x 2.8 x 2.3 cm
Polymer clay, hematite spacers; hollow
formed with millefiori elements
PHOTOGRAPHY BY DOUG YAPLE

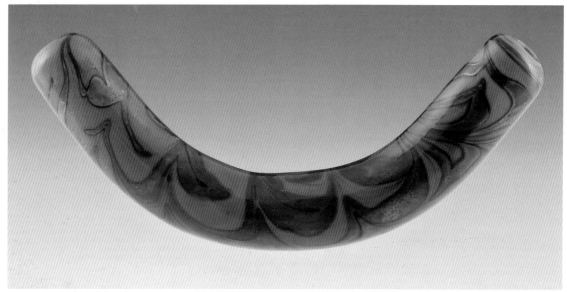

TOP
MARADA GENZ
Frozen Rainbow ■ 2013
1 x 3 x 3 cm
Polymer clay; formed, cured, sanded
PHOTOGRAPHY BY ARTIST

BOTTOM
PATRICIA WESTBY
Frosted Sherbet Half Marbled ■ 2013
3.8 x 8.4 x 1.3 cm
Soda-lime glass; flameworked
PHOTOGRAPHY BY ANN CADY

ESTHER HSING-LING LIAO
The Remained ■ 2013

Dimensions vary
Transparent plastic water pipe, lacquer
and acrylic paints; cut, heat shaped
PHOTOGRAPHY BY ARTIST

LESLIE KAPLAN
Seashell ■ 2012
19 x 3 x 0.5 cm
Borosilicate glass; flameworked, sandblasted
PHOTOGRAPHY BY LARRY BERMAN

HAROLD COONEY

New Hampshire Trade Beads ■ 2013

Dimensions vary
Glass; lampworked, lapidary techniques
PHOTOGRAPHY BY KONNIE SMART

TRISTYN ALBRIGHT
Untitled ■ 2012

Each bead: 3.5 x 3.5 x 3.5 cm
Copper wire, glass beads; spoke wrapped
PHOTOGRAPHY BY ARTIST

MURIEL DUVAL
Sea Garden ■ 2012
1.3 x 1.3 x 0.5 cm
Soft glass; flameworked, murrini
PHOTOGRAPHY BY ARTIST

STEPHANIE SERSICH
Caged Bead ■ 2013
3.8 x 3.8 x 3.8 cm
African glass, seed beads; lampworked, sewn
PHOTOGRAPHY BY TOM EICHLER

GALINA GREBENNIKOVA
Irish Blessing ■ 2012

Dimensions vary
Polymer clay; stamped, textured
PHOTOGRAPHY BY ARTIST

LAURA BOWKER
Shifting Groove ■ 2012

3.1 x 3.8 cm
Glass; battuto engraved, flameworked
PHOTOGRAPHY BY ARTIST

1000
beads

PATTY LAKINSMITH
Vibrant Trio ■ 2013
Left: 3.7 x 1.6 cm; center: 5.5 x 1.7 cm; right: 4.5 x 2.2 cm
Soda-lime glass; flameworked
PHOTOGRAPHY BY DAVID ORR

NIINA MAHLBERG
Cups ■ 2012
Each bead: 1.5 x 2 x 2 cm
Ceramic; cast
PHOTOGRAPHY BY ARTIST

MARTA BERNBAUM
Bamboo ■ 2012
4.5 x 1.5 x 1.5 cm
Glass, enamel, mixed media; flameworked, strung
PHOTOGRAPHY BY JOHN POLAK

TOM FINNERAN
Totem 10 ■ 2012
9.1 x 1.4 x 0.9 cm
British Columbian nephrite jade;
milled, lapidary techniques
PHOTOGRAPHY BY DAVE BURCHETT

SANDRA LENT
Twilight Butterflies ■ 2012
6 x 40 x 0.5 cm
Glass; flameworked, acid etched, assembled

KIMBERLY ARDEN
Grande Collar ▦ 2013

66 x 22.8 cm
Polymer clay, metal disks, sterling silver
PHOTOGRAPHY BY ERICKA CRISSMAN

161

SZILVIA VIHRIÄLÄ
Mind Swirl Beads ■ 2012

Each: 2 x 2 x 0.8 cm
Hand-formed and carved white earthenware, glazes; electric
fired, cone 09, refired in sauna stove, cone 06, saggar fired

BRENDA SCHLEGEL
Geometric Patina Beads ■ 2013

Largest bead: 1 x 2.2 cm
Copper, silver, bronze, patina; saw pierced, appliquéd,
molded, cast, assembled, riveted, waxed
PHOTOGRAPHY BY MARIA SCHLEGEL

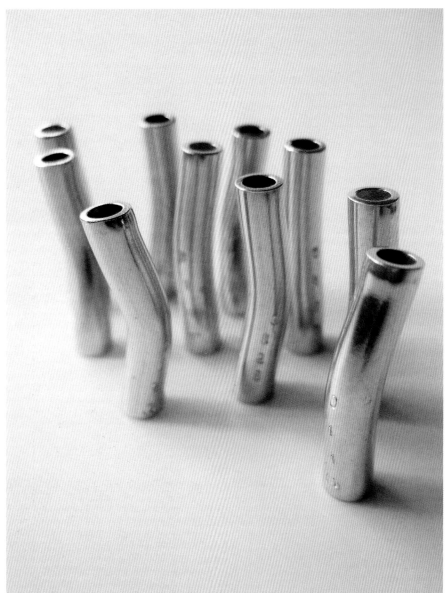

ESTHER HSING-LING LIAO
The Suit ■ 2013

Dimensions vary
Aluminum; hand sewn, stamped, die
formed, sanded, polished
PHOTOGRAPHY BY THE ARTIST

KARI WOO
Reversible Bead Pendants ■ 2011

Largest: 3.5 x 2 x 0.5 cm
Sterling silver; lost wax cast, drilled
PHOTOGRAPHY BY ARTIST

MEGAN PARKS
The Universe ■ 2012

22 x 1.8 x 1.8 cm
Beads; peyote stitch
PHOTOGRAPHY BY SUSAN EWERT

LINDA HUEY
Handmade-Factory Made ■ 2011

Overall length: 71 cm
Low-fire ceramic, commercial metal and rubber
parts, commercial glass and bone beads
PHOTOGRAPHY BY MARIKA BURKE

LUCIE KOVAROVA-WEIR
Life in a Country Series ■ 2013
Dimensions vary
Glass; flameworked
PHOTOGRAPHY BY ARTIST

CLAIRE MORRIS
Celtic Tree ■ 2012
4 x 3 x 11 cm
Soda-lime glass, silver; flameworked, stringer application
PHOTOGRAPHY BY ARTIST

KRISTEN FRANTZEN ORR
Bon Appetit ▪ 2010
43 x 2.5 x 2.5 cm
Soda-lime glass, Japanese seed beads, brass accent beads, sterling silver end
caps, peppercorns, mustard seeds, copper wire; flameworked, crocheted
PHOTOGRAPHY BY DAVID ORR

MAUREEN HENRIQUES
Sand Dollars ■ 2012

Each: 2 x 2 x 0.5 cm
Soda-lime glass; flameworked, murrini, etched
PHOTOGRAPHY BY ARTIST

CARISSA NICHOLS
Steampunk Flower ■ 2012

9 x 9 x 3.5 cm
Polymer clay, mica powders, cabachon; hand sculpted
PHOTOGRAPHY BY KATHY DUMMER

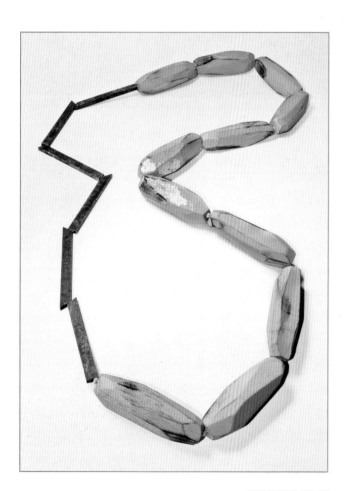

CRISTINA ZANI
My Seoul Yellow and Patina Necklace ■ 2012
36 x 9 x 3 cm
Brass, wood, acrylic paint, patina, 24-karat gold leaf,
linen thread; sanded, burned, fabricated, threaded
PHOTOGRAPHY BY ARTIST

ROMY MITTELMAN
A Memoir ■ 2011
Overall length: 90 cm
Film canisters, glue; oxidized, formed, threaded
PHOTOGRAPHY BY JOHN BRASH

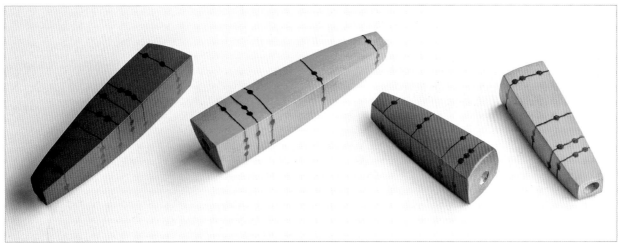

KIMBERLY WINKLE
Faceted Wrapped Beads ■ 2013

Largest bead: 1 x 1 x 6 cm
Poplar beads, milk paint, hand-drawn
embellishments; hand shaped
PHOTOGRAPHY BY BEN CORDA

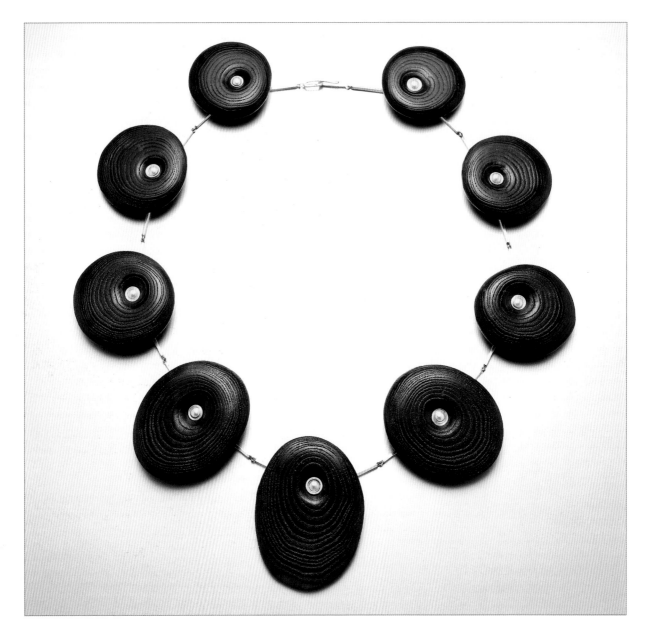

DANIEL RANDALL
Untitled ■ 2013

22 x 20 x 2 cm
Wood, sterling silver; carved,
burned, fabricated
PHOTOGRAPHY BY KC STUDIO

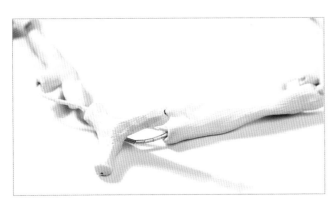

LAUREN SIMEONI
Stick Building Lei—White ■ 2013
42 x 20 x 2 cm
Hand-built porcelain, glass, howlite, sterling
silver, artificial plant foliage
PHOTOGRAPHY BY CRAIG ARNOLD

LAUREN SIMEONI
Stick Building Lei—Black ■ 2013
38 x 22 x 2.5 cm
Hand-built porcelain, sterling silver, black stone, larvikite, howlite,
glass beads, plastic beads, artificial plant foliage; oxidized
PHOTOGRAPHY BY CRAIG ARNOLD

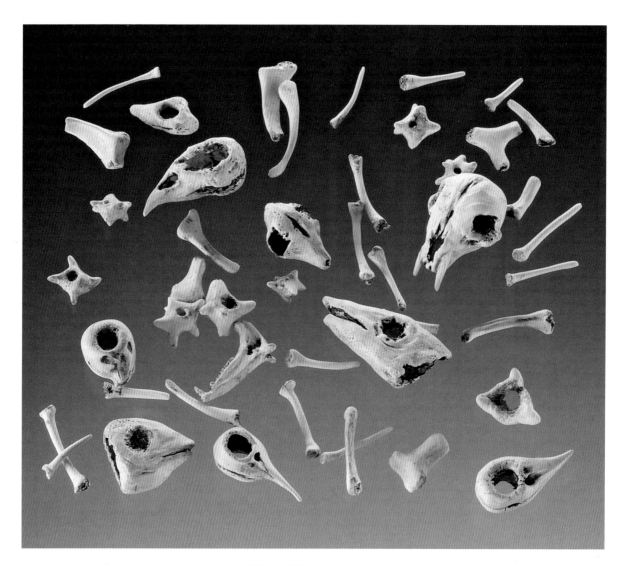

WENDY MALINOW
Bone Party ■ 2013

Largest bead: 5.1 x 3.8 cm
Polymer, acrylic patina; hollow
formed, sculpted, cured, buffed
PHOTOGRAPHY BY COURTNEY FRISSE

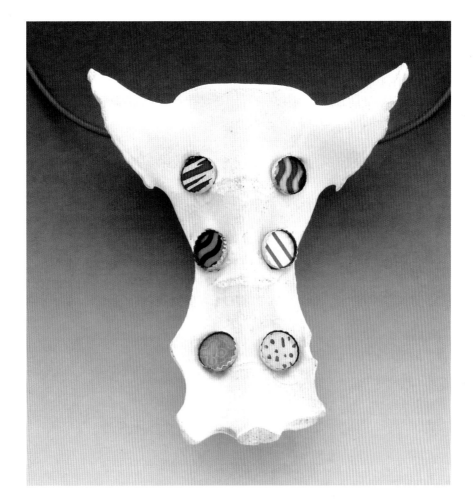

REBECCA MCLAUGHLIN NEIGHER
Georgia on My Mind ■ 2013
10 x 7.5 x 3.5 cm
Found bone, anodized aluminum, sterling silver,
fine silver, leather, cement; soldered
PHOTOGRAPHY BY ARTIST

KAZUHIRO TAJIKA
Goldfishes ■ 2012
29.5 x 35 x 30 cm
Glass; flameworked
PHOTOGRAPHY BY TAKAYUKI MATSUZAWA

SHERRY BELLAMY
Tapestry Kelp ■ 2012
1.4 x 1.2 x 0.7 cm
Glass, silver wire; flameworked, knotted
PHOTOGRAPHY BY ARTIST

TANYA LYONS
Wish Bead ■ 2013
2.9 x 3 x 2.9 cm
Glass beads, dandelion seeds; flameworked
PHOTOGRAPHY BY ARTIST

AYELET LINDENSTRAUSS LARSEN
Two Hyperbolic Annuli, Different Curvatures ■ 2013

0.8 x 1.5 x 1.5 cm
Cotton thread; crochet
PHOTOGRAPHY BY ARTIST

ELIANE ROEMER
Sensation ■ 2013

45 x 20 x 15 cm
Sterling silver, pearls, fabric, polyester fiberfill,
elastic cord; formed, soldered, riveted, strung
PHOTOGRAPHY BY JOSÉ TERRA

DOUG BALDWIN
Leopard Bead Set ■ 2011
12.5 x 2.5 x 2.5 cm
Borosilicate glass; flameworked
PHOTOGRAPHY BY ARTIST

MAUREEN CHIN
Cool Summer Wave ■ 2012
4 x 4 x 2.5 cm
Japanese glass seed beads and glass drops, Czech glass
seed beads and glass drops; peyote stitch, embellished
PHOTOGRAPHY BY ARTIST

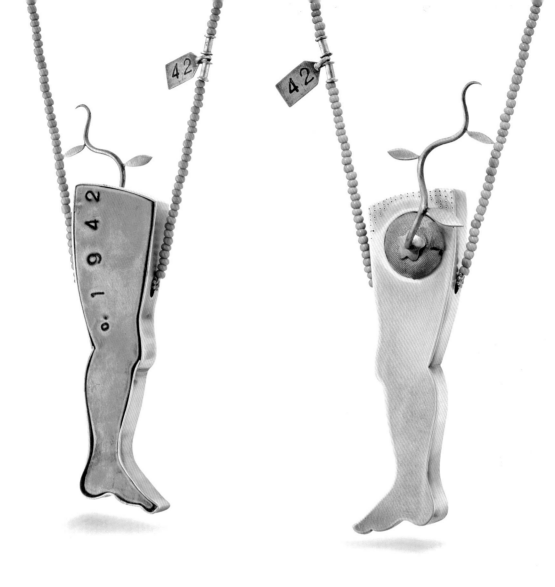

LEAH HARDY
c. 1942 ■ 2012

42 x 4 x 2.5 cm
Vintage seed beads, sterling silver, brass,
copper, glazed fabric, patina; fabricated
PHOTOGRAPHY BY HAP SAKWA

183

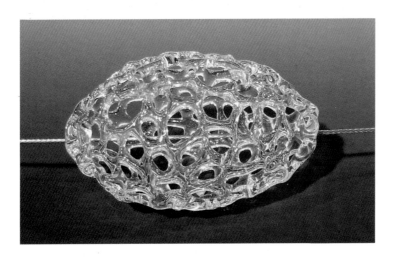

DONNA PRUNKARD
Lace in Glass ■ 2013
3.2 x 4.5 x 3.2 cm
Borosilicate glass; networking technique
PHOTOGRAPHY BY ARTIST

EMMA BOURKE
Foxglove Beads ■ 2012
20 x 16 x 5 cm
Borosilicate glass; flameworked, sandblasted
PHOTOGRAPHY BY ARTIST

CYNTHIA TOOPS
Hey Diddle Diddle ■ 2012

56 x 4.5 x 1.3 cm
Polymer clay, glass, enamel, silver; micro-mosaic,
lampworked, cane work, carved
LAMPWORKED GLASS BY DAN ADAMS
PHOTOGRAPHY BY DOUG YAPLE

185

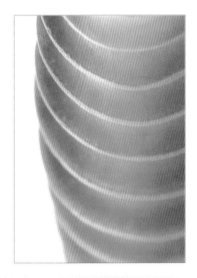

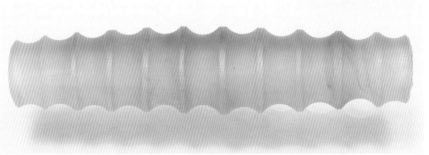

IVONNE PALACIOS
Fertility ■ 2012
5 x 5 x 5 cm
Merino wool, silk; hand dyed, wet felted
PHOTOGRAPHY BY ARTIST

MARTA EDÖCS
Harmony ■ 2012
1 x 6 x 1 cm
Soda-lime glass; flameworked,
fire polished, ground
PHOTOGRAPHY BY ESZTER GALAMBOS

1000
beads

STEPHANIE SERSICH
Felted Beads ■ 2013

Left: 3.3 x 3.5 x 3.5 cm; right: 3.3 x 9 x 3.3 cm
Wool, glass, seed beads, sequins;
felted, flameworked, sewn
PHOTOGRAPHY BY TOM EICHLER

KELLY ROBERGE
Garden Beads ■ 2012
10 x 2 x 2 cm
Wool; needle felted, wet felted
PHOTOGRAPHY BY GREG SAWYER

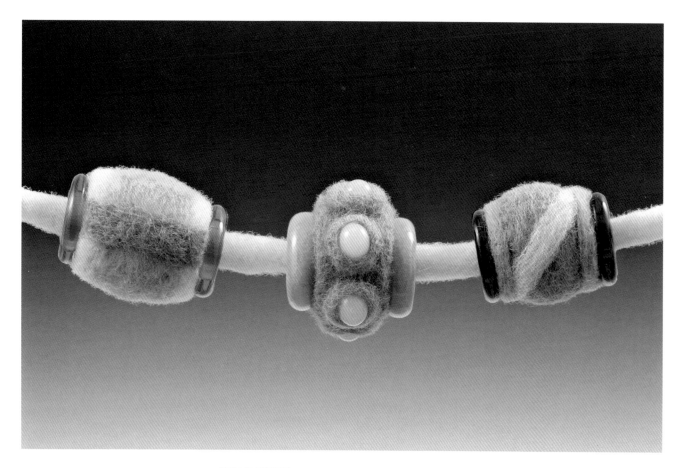

EVE NAGODE
Felted Glass Spools ■ 2013

Each: 3.2 x 2.5 x 2.5 cm
Glass, Czech glass drop beads, wool roving, plastic
tubing; hand dyed, lampworked, needle and wet felted
PHOTOGRAPHY BY ARTIST

SOGANG JEON
Marble 2 ■ 2012
46 x 12 x 3.5 cm
Glass, plastic straw, brass, resin, paint; melted
PHOTOGRAPHY BY MUNCH STUDIO

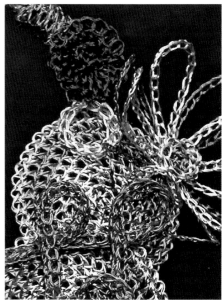

YU LIN LIN
Flower Garden ■ 2012
3 x 40 x 35 cm
Silver-plated copper wire; weaving techniques
PHOTOGRAPHY BY ARTIST

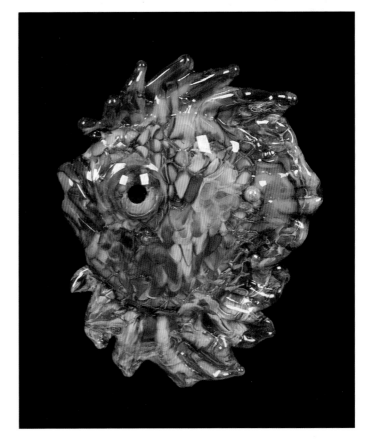

PATTY LAKINSMITH
Encased and Twisted Bicone ■ 2010
2 x 0.8 x cm
Soda-lime glass; flameworked
PHOTOGRAPHY BY DAVID ORR

PATSY EVINS
Kaleidoscope Discus Fish ■ 2011
5.6 x 4.4 x 1.5 cm
Soda-lime glass, copper mesh wire; flameworked
PHOTOGRAPHY BY CHRISTOPHER EVINS

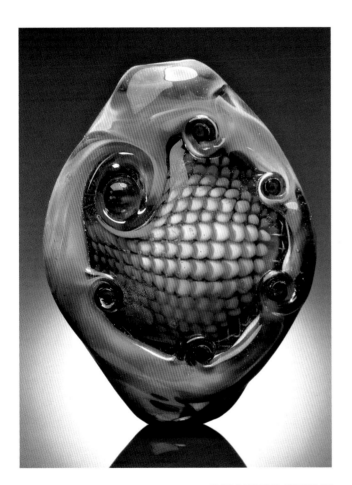

SHELLEY MCLAUGHLIN
Hot Lava ■ 2012
3.5 x 5 x 1.5 cm
Soda-lime glass, copper mesh; flameworked
PHOTOGRAPHY BY DAVID ORR

KATHRYN GULER
Cosmic Collision Saguaro ■ 2011
3 x 2 x 0.5 cm
Soda-lime glass, silver foil, enamel, steel
wire; flameworked, stringer work
PHOTOGRAPHY BY DAVID ORR

HOLLY KELLOGG
Lentil Beads ■ 2013
Each: 8 x 10 x 3 cm
Metal clay, patina; textured
PHOTOGRAPHY BY ARTIST

TRACY DIPIAZZA
Steel Shaving Bead ■ 2013
1.5 x 3.5 x 1.5 cm
Lead-free pewter, steel; fused, soldered
PHOTOGRAPHY BY ARTIST

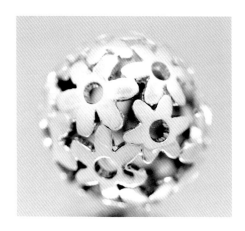

WIWAT KAMOLPORNWIJIT
Rose Petals ■ 2013
2 x 24 x 0.4 cm
Polymer clay; hand formed, layered, sliced
PHOTOGRAPHY BY ARTIST

MARIEL PAGLIAI
Florentina ■ 2013
3 x 3 x 3 cm
Sterling silver; handmade
PHOTOGRAPHY BY ARTIST

MIRIAM PAPPALARDO
Jornal Beads ■ 2010

Each bead: 2 x 2 cm; necklace: 25 x 18 x 3 cm
Newspaper; cut
PHOTOGRAPHY BY ARTIST

LILY LIU
PB2 ■ 2013
9 x 11 x 11 cm
Marbled paper, cardstock, copper,
aluminum; hand cut, tube riveted
PHOTOGRAPHY BY ARTIST

BLAKE WILLIAMS
AMY BROWN
Petal Confetti: Rose Fan Necklace ■ 2012
Overall length: 45.7 cm; each bead: 2.5 x 2.5 cm
Porcelain, glass, silver; hand built, stained
PHOTOGRAPHY BY TIM THAYER

ALICE KRESSE
Orange Paper Beads ■ 2013
Each bead: 2.5 x 3.8 cm
Polyester, sterling silver tube; hand
painted, cut, assembled, dapped
PHOTOGRAPHY BY ARTIST

MICHOU PASCALE ANDERSON
Cosmic World ■ 2012

Dimensions vary
Glass; flameworked, etched
PHOTOGRAPHY BY ARTIST

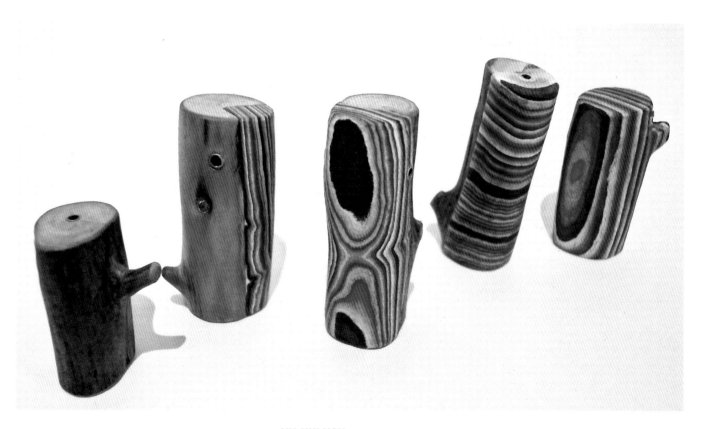

YU-HUI HSU
Wood and Paper ■ 2013

Dimensions vary
Wood, paper, brass; cut, mosaic
PHOTOGRAPHY BY ARTIST

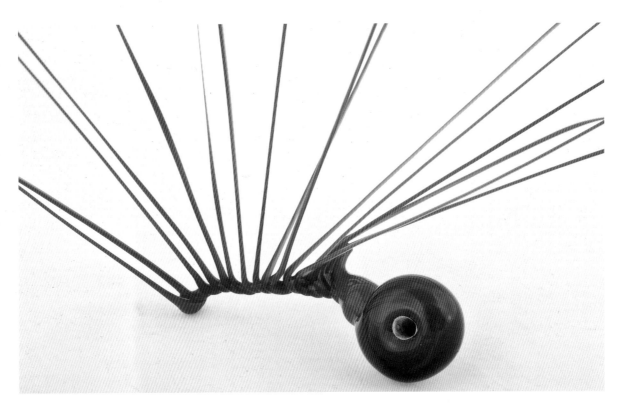

REUT TRAUM
Electrified Bead ■ 2013
25 x 25 x 6 cm
Glass; flameworked
PHOTOGRAPHY BY ANNA OHANA

EVE NAGODE
Heartthrob Spool Bead ▪ 2013

2.5 x 3.2 x 2.5 cm
Glass, magatama beads, sead beads, carpet thread;
lampworked, ladder-stitch, kumihimo braiding
PHOTOGRAPHY BY ARTIST

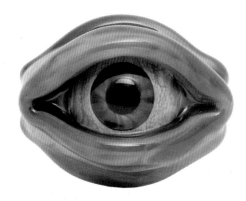

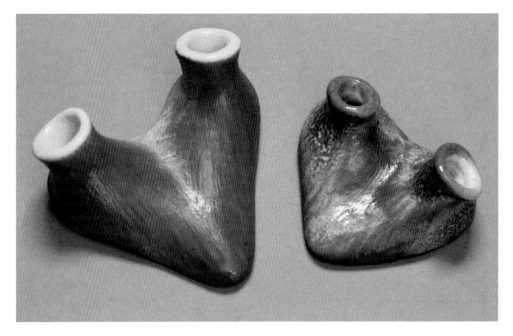

JANEL DUDLEY
Evil-Eye Focal ■ 2013
2.2 x 2.9 x 2.2 cm
Soda-lime glass; flameworked, murrini
PHOTOGRAPHY BY ARTIST

DEBRA EVANS-PAIGE
Heart Series ■ 2012
Left: 7.3 x 7.8 x 3.3 cm
Right: 5.4 x 6.4 x 2.9 cm
Hand-built porcelain; soda fired
PHOTOGRAPHY BY ARTIST

MARION DELARUE
Amulet Set of Jewelry ■ 2010

Each: 2.5 x 2.5 x 2.5 cm
Glass; flameworked
PHOTOGRAPHY BY ARTIST

KATIE GOLDEN
Kundalini Rising ■ 2012

84 x 2 x 1.5 cm
Soda-lime glass, cotton; flameworked,
braided, fine-ash annealed
PHOTOGRAPHY BY ALESSANDRO CASTAGNA

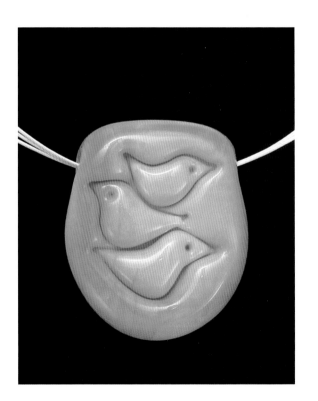

GILA FOX
Mango Trio ■ 2012
2.8 x 2.5 x 0.9 cm
Soda-lime glass, hand-made stamps; flameworked
PHOTOGRAPHY BY TIM FOX

MATHIEU GRODET
Honey Cone ■ 2013
3.6 x 2 x 2 cm
Glass; flameworked
PHOTOGRAPHY BY TANYA LYONS

KATRINA VIRGONA
Psychonautics ■ 2013

17 x 46 x 5 cm; largest bead: 5 cm in diameter
Silk, cotton and synthetic threads;
hand fabricated, stitched
PHOTOGRAPHY BY BEN JOEL

FABIENNE SCHALLER
Le Rouge ■ 2011

Each bead: 2 x 2 x 2 cm
Merino wool, cotton thread; wet felted,
hand shaped, embroidered, embellished
PHOTOGRAPHY BY MARY KNIGHT AND ARTIST

JERI WARHAFTIG
Yummy Wafer ■ 2012

Largest bead: 2.5 x 2.5 x 0.9 cm
Glass; flameworked, embellished
with original sandblasted design
PHOTOGRAPHY BY PANOS LAMBROU

SANDRA REICH
Holly, Hellebore, and Poinsettia ■ 2012
3.2 x 3.2 x 3.2 cm
Soda-lime glass; lampworked, murrini
PHOTOGRAPHY BY ARTIST

HELEN MOORE
Mandevilla ■ 2013
Each bead: 2.1 x 1.6 cm
Soda-lime glass, Swarovski crystals, sterling
silver chain; lampworked, encased
PHOTOGRAPHY BY ARTIST

MEGAN BOGONOVICH
Big Masculine Necklace ■ 2011

Overall length: 180 cm
Slip-cast ceramic, low-fire glaze decoration
PHOTOGRAPHY BY CHARLEY FREIBERG

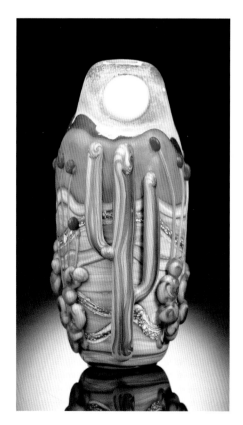

DIANE SEPANSKI
Arizona Dreams ■ 2012
1 x 0.5 x 0.5 cm
Soft glass; flameworked, etched
PHOTOGRAPHY BY DAVID ORR

SHER BERMAN
Turquoise Dots ■ 2013
2 x 0.7 x 0.5 cm
Soda-lime glass, enamel powders, copper
leaf, silver foil; stringer application, etched
PHOTOGRAPHY BY LARRY SANDERS

AURELIO CASTANO
Iraca Beads ■ 2010

Each: 0.8 x 1 x 1 cm
Iraca palm wood from Colombia; basketry technique
PHOTOGRAPHY BY ARTIST

JULIE LONG GALLEGOS
Beaded Beads for an Easter Bracelet ■ 2013

Each: 2.5 x 2 x 2 cm
Japanese glass seed beads, coral, freshwater pearl,
carnelian and aventurine beads; beadweaving
PHOTOGRAPHY BY GEORGE POST

MARIANNE KELLEY
The Roman ■ 2013
3 x 2 x 2 cm
Glass, diamond bits; blown,
flameworked, engraved, polished
PHOTOGRAPHY BY ANN CADY

MENG CHIEH WEI
Telescope ■ 2013
9 x 10 x 20 cm
Glass, aluminum alloy; fired
PHOTOGRAPHY BY ARTIST

JOELLE SHAFTER
Jewels of the sea ■ 2013
Dimensions vary
Felt, freshwater pearls; rolled, beaded, crocheted
PHOTOGRAPHY BY ALEXANDRA SHAFTER

GALIT EINAV
Mystery ■ 2013
1.5 x 1.5 x 8 cm
Enamel beads; knit
PHOTOGRAPHY BY AMOS TRABOLSKY

SUSAN HOOD
Phantasea Shell ■ 2012

5 x 5 x 4 cm
Soda-lime glass; flameworked
PHOTOGRAPHY BY MEGAN ELEMENT

BARBARA SIMON
Aqua Big-Hole Bead ■ 2010
3 x 3 x 1 cm
Soft glass, silver metal clay armature
PHOTOGRAPHY BY BABETTE BELMONDO

LYNNE GLAZZARD
Koi Bead ■ 2012
3 x 2 x 2 cm
Silver precious metal clay, fine silver, enamel; constructed, fired
PHOTOGRAPHY BY ARTIST

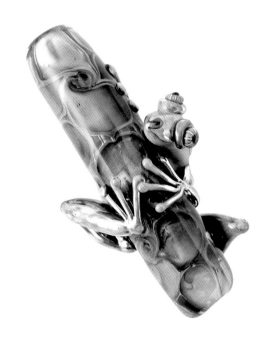

CORINA TETTINGER
Curiosity Killed No Frog ■ 2012
2.5 x 1 x 0.8 cm
Soda-lime glass; flameworked
PHOTOGRAPHY BY ARTIST

LIBBY LEUCHTMAN
Cold-Worked Cane Disk ■ 2012
4 x 4 x 2 cm
Glass; flameworked, murrini, cold worked
PHOTOGRAPHY BY ARTIST

KENNETH MACBAIN
Bead Necklace ■ 2013

Bead: 8 x 3 x 2 cm
Copper, 24-karat gold leaf, resin, leather
cord; die formed, hollow constructed

ADRIENNE GASKELL
Jewels in a Box Necklace ■ 2011
2.8 x 0.8 x 30 cm
Japanese glass seed beads, Swarovski crystals;
needle beadweaving, kumihimo braiding
PHOTOGRAPHY BY HAP SAKWA

ROMY MITTELMAN
A Drunken Night out ■ 2012

Overall length: 74 cm
Discarded bottle tops, sterling silver,
enamel paint; threaded, oxidized
PHOTOGRAPHY BY PIECES OF EIGHT GALLERY

KIMBERLY WINKLE
Wooden Ruffle Beaded Necklace ■ 2013

Overall length: 51 cm
Cherry-wood beads, hand-drawn
embellishments; hand shaped and textured
PHOTOGRAPHY BY BEN CORDA

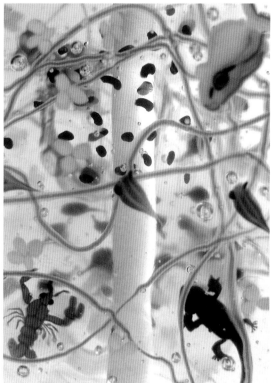

MASAE NAKAHARA
In the Pond ■ 2012
3.8 x 3.7 x 1.9 cm
Soda-lime glass; lampworked, millefiori
PHOTOGRAPHY BY ARTIST

NELL BURNS
English Garden Embroidered Bead ▨ 2013
1.5 x 0.7 x 0.2 cm
Silk, beads; hand and freestyle machine embroidered

TAMAR GLICK
Leather Beads ▪ 2011
20 x 20 x 20 cm
Leather, silver; hand fabricated
PHOTOGRAPHY BY MOR ELNEKAVE

BRIGIT DAAMEN
Giant Necklace ▪ 2004
Overall length: 125 cm
Merino wool, plastic beads; felted
PHOTOGRAPHY BY ARTIST

MENGNAN QU
One Thousand Beads ■ 2013
13 x 6 x 2 cm
Copper, enamel; overglazed
PHOTOGRAPHY BY YU XIA

MELANIE MOERTEL
Clear Lakes ■ 2012

Each bead: 2.5 x 2.5 x 1 cm
Glass; flameworked,
stringer application

DONNA MILLARD
Tango ■ 2012

Largest bead: 1.8 x 1.8 x 1.8 cm
Soda-lime glass; etched, stringer work
PHOTOGRAPHY BY ARTIST

ALISA LETCIUS
African Tree Beads ■ 2012

Each bead: 3 x 4 x 2 cm
Polymer clay, wax cord,
epoxy; hand shaped, baked
PHOTOGRAPHY BY ARTIST

MICHELE COLETTI
The Perfect Bead ▓ 2012
3.3 x 0.3 x 0.3 cm
Soda-lime glass; flameworked
PHOTOGRAPHY BY DAVID ORR

CANDACE STRIBLING
Lampworked Paper Bead ▓ 2013
1 x 0.1 x 0.1 cm
Joss paper, paint, adhesive; carved, sealed
PHOTOGRAPHY BY ADHESIVE

KATHRYN GULER
Cosmic Collision Series ■ 2012
2.3 x 1.8 x 0.8 cm
Soda-lime glass, silver foil, enamel;
flameworked, stringer work
PHOTOGRAPHY BY DAVID ORR

ALISA LETCIUS
Hundertwasser Beads ■ 2011

0.5 x 40 x 6 cm

Polymer clay, wax cord, gold and
silver leaf; hand shaped, baked
PHOTOGRAPHY BY ARTIST

235

EVE NAGODE
Sea Urchin Spool Bead ■ 2013
3.8 x 3.5 x 3.8 cm
Glass, seed beads, dagger beads;
lampworked, peyote stitch, whip stitch
PHOTOGRAPHY BY ARTIST

KARMEN SCHMIDT
Flights of Fancy I ■ 2013
7.5 x 4 x 4 cm
Polyethylene tubing, Czech dagger beads, peanut
beads, Japanese seed beads; peyote stitch, netting
PHOTOGRAPHY BY KAREN BETTIN

BECKY FAIRCLOUGH
Ode to Miss Haversham ▩ 2012

Each: 2 x 2 x 0.8 cm
Soda-lime glass, enamel transfers,
luster, cubic zirconia; flameworked
PHOTOGRAPHY BY ARTIST

YONE PANELLA
Fragments Necklace ■ 2012

34 x 26 cm
Papier-mâché, sterling silver,
silk thread; handmade
PHOTOGRAPHY BY JOSÉ TERRA

MICHAELA MARIA MOELLER
Untitled ■ 2012
3 x 3 x 45 cm
Glass, gold plate, custom-made
rubber; flameworked, engraved
PHOTOGRAPHY BY ARTIST

TRACY DIPIAZZA
Steel and Spiral Bead ■ 2013
3.5 x 3.5 x 3.3 cm
Lead-free pewter, steel, sterling silver,
bronze, brass; dap formed, fused, soldered
PHOTOGRAPHY BY ARTIST

SO YOUNG PARK
Oriental Hill II ■ 2011
15 x 15 x 1.5 cm
Silver, 24-karat yellow gold leaf, freshwater pearls; oxidized,
hand fabricated, hammered, soldered, hand engraved
PHOTOGRAPHY BY ARTIST

ISABELLE POSILLICO
Lava Beads with 18-Karat Time Ribbon Bead ■ 2010

1.3 x 19 x 1.3 cm
18-karat gold, lava beads; rollerprinted, constructed, soldered
PHOTOGRAPHY BY HAP SAKWA

CRISTINA DIAS
Criatura Beads ■ 2010

Dimensions vary
Silicone rubber, pigment, wool,
fiber, wire; constructed, coated
PHOTOGRAPHY BY ARTIST

JACQUELINE HUGHES
Mutation Bead Series 2 ■ 2012
4 x 12 x 16 cm
Low-fire white clay, china paint, low-fire glaze
PHOTOGRAPHY BY ARTIST

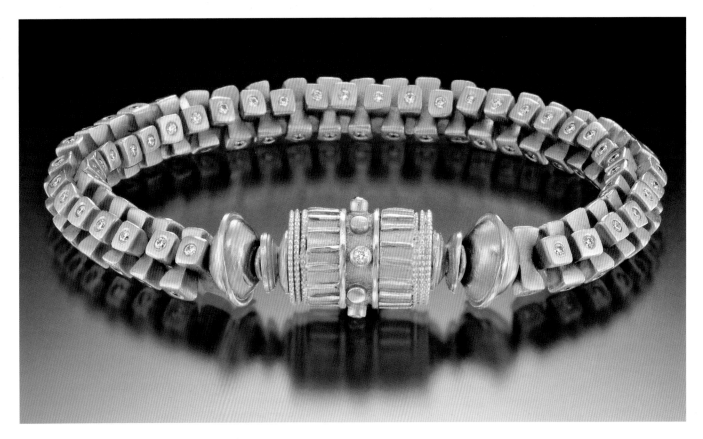

JUDITH KAUFMAN
Vertebra Bracelet ■ 2011

0.5 x 7 x 0.5 cm
Diamonds, 14-karat rose gold, 18-karat
green gold, 22-karat yellow gold

1000
beads

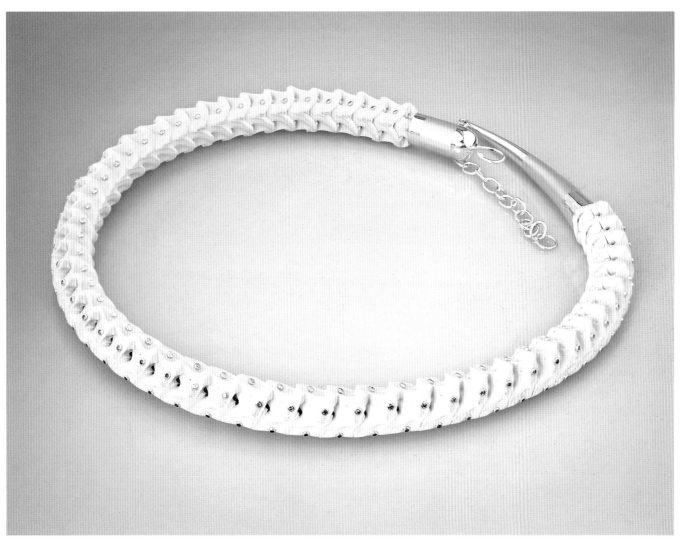

GERMAN KABIRSKI
Cobra Backbone Necklace ▨ 2012

15.6 x 15.6 cm
Cobra backbone, gold, diamonds; soldered, engraved
PHOTOGRAPHY BY ANDREY KULKOV

JENNIFER FITZGERALD
Three Nests ■ 2012

7.6 x 17.8 x 6.4 cm
Wheel-thrown ceramic; glazed
with oxides, reduction fired
PHOTOGRAPHY BY ARTIST

MELISSA GRAKOWSKY SHIPPEE
Acorn Beads ■ 2013

Large bead: 2.8 x 2.6 x 2.6 cm; small bead: 2.5 x 2 x 2 cm
Oak seeds, aluminum tubing, nickel plate;
glued, hammered, cut, drilled
PHOTOGRAPHY BY ARTIST

DORIS HÄUSLER
Book Beads ■ 2013

Left: 5 x 2.5 cm; center: 5.2 x 2 cm; right: 2.2 cm in diameter
Book spines, book pages; cut, glued, varnished
PHOTOGRAPHY BY ARTIST

BARBARA SIMON
Info Beads ■ 2009
Round bead: 2.5 x 2.5 cm
Soft glass, glass paint; sgrafitto
PHOTOGRAPHY BY LARRY SANDERS

BONNIE POLINSKI
Blue Daisy ■ 2012
3.2 x 2.1 x 1.3 cm
Clay, glaze, sterling silver wire and scraps; raku
fired, soldered, silversmithing techniques
PHOTOGRAPHY BY ARTIST

TRACEY BROOME
Raku Beads ■ 2012
Each: 0.7 x 3 cm
Stoneware clay, copper carbonate glaze, clay
stamp; raku fired, reduction cooled
PHOTOGRAPHY BY ARTIST

NANCY SCHINDLER
Persian Box Beads ■ 2012

Each bead: 2.5 x 5.1 cm
Hand-built porcelain; embossed
PHOTOGRAPHY BY ARTIST

KELLY ROBERGE
Bone Beads ■ 2013
Each bead: 6.5 x 2 x 1 cm
Graphite transfer on polymer clay
PHOTOGRAPHY BY ARTIST

GERMAN KABIRSKI
Skull Beads Necklace ■ 2012
13.9 x 13.9 x 24 cm
Ivory, gold, diamonds; engraved
PHOTOGRAPHY BY ANDREY KULKOV

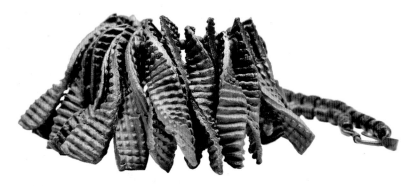

PAJA VAN DYCK
Just Sitting ■ 2011

45 x 4 x 4 cm
Soda-lime glass, copper;
flameworked, electroformed
PHOTOGRAPHY BY ARTIST

BARBARA HANSELMAN
Textured Twists Neckwear ■ 2012

Each twisted bead: 5.7 x 1.2 cm; overall length: 60.9 cm
Stoneware clay, African sand beads, glass seed beads; hand
formed, terra sigillata, electric fired, cone 5/6, assembled
PHOTOGRAPHY BY GLENN HUDSON

CYNTHIA TOOPS
Tubes ■ 2012
51 x 5 x 1.3 cm
Polymer clay, sterling silver
PHOTOGRAPHY BY DOUG YAPLE

255

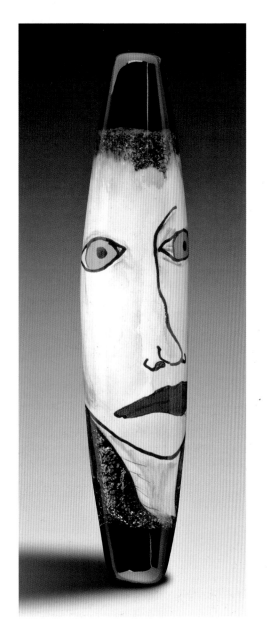

BRONWEN HEILMAN
Princess ■ 2010
3.5 x 0.5 x 0.5 cm
Glass, enamel; flameworked
PHOTOGRAPHY BY DOUG BALDWIN

LAURIE GELLER
Igor ■ 2012
6.2 x 6.3 cm
Glass; flameworked, kiln annealed, stringer work
PHOTOGRAPHY BY ARTIST

1000
beads

SHARON PETERS
Maya Spike Bead ▪ 2013
15 x 2.5 x 0.8 cm
Soda-lime glass, steel spikes, Swarovski rondelles,
silver findings, epoxy; flameworked
PHOTOGRAPHY BY JIM TRENKLE

RONIT DAGAN
From the Mystery of the Turning Bead Series ▪ 2011
22 x 6 x 6 cm
Borosilicate glass, oil paint; flameworked, blown, sandblasted
PHOTOGRAPHY BY LEONID PADRUL

VALERIA DOWDING
Piñatas ■ 2013
Each bead: 10 x 8.5 x 8.5 cm
Tissue paper, cotton string, glue; hand formed

JENNY KEYSER
Gyro Necklace ■ 2013
7.6 x 1.3 cm
Wooden bead, sterling silver
chain; cut, sealed, wired

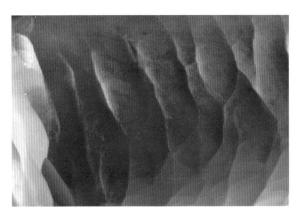

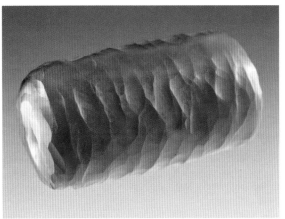

MARIANNE KELLEY
Green Sea ■ 2012
1.6 x 2.9 x 1.6 cm
Glass; flameworked, engraved, polished
PHOTOGRAPHY BY ANN CADY

DIANA FERGUSON
Scroll Bead Neckpiece ■ 2012
5 x 3.5 x 1.5 cm
Polymer clay, watercolor paper, poly-acrylic, stainless
steel cord; digital transfer, hand sculpted, collaged
PHOTOGRAPHY BY LARRY SANDERS

MIGUEL DE DIEGO
Mil Gotas de Color (One Thousand Colored Drops) ▦ 2011
4 x 1.5 x 4 cm
Soda-lime glass, rubber; flameworked
PHOTOGRAPHY BY SONIA OSUNA

BARBARA FAJARDO
Constellations ▦ 2013
Each: 1.5 x 1.5 x 0.3 cm
Polymer clay, alcohol inks, paint
PHOTOGRAPHY BY ARTIST

ANNE-LISE MEIER
Dot by Dot ■ 2013
Each: 2.1 x 2.1 x 2.1 cm
Glass, luster; flameworked
PHOTOGRAPHY BY ARTIST

LISA ATCHISON
Electroformed and Etched Focal ■ 2012
5.8 x 3.3 x 1.5 cm
Soda-lime glass, silver leaf, copper, cubic zirconias, patina;
flameworked, cane work, electroformed, etched
PHOTOGRAPHY BY ARTIST

LISA ST. MARTIN
Swirl Dichro Bead ■ 2010
2.8 x 1 x 1 cm
Soda-lime glass; flameworked, carved
PHOTOGRAPHY BY JERRY ANTHONY

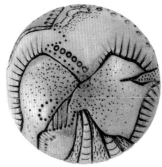

LYNNE SWARD
Stained Glass ■ 2013

6.3 x 3.5 x 0.7 cm
Metallic and cotton fabrics, interfacing, glass
and metal beads; hand and machine sewn
PHOTOGRAPHY BY JEFFREY ALLEN DIENER

PATTY PULLIAM
Dawn ■ 2012

4.5 x 2.3 x 2.3 cm
Polymer clay, acrylic paint;
blended, incised, antiqued
PHOTOGRAPHY BY ARTIST

263

KIMBERLY ARDEN
Necklace ■ 2010

50.8 x 5.1 cm
Polymer clay, gemstones, sterling silver
PHOTOGRAPHY BY ERICKA CRISSMAN

VANESSA HEARN
Puzzlewood ■ 2012

0.2 x 0.2 x 0.1 cm
Soft glass, fine silver leaf, copper,
leaf enamels; flameworked
PHOTOGRAPHY BY ARTIST

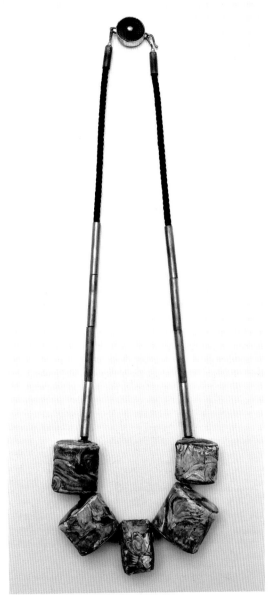

MICKI LIPPE
Bark Beads ■ 2012

33 x 2 x 1 cm
Reclaimed sterling silver, polyester
cord, carnelian; fabricated
PHOTOGRAPHY BY ARTIST

BRONWYNN LUSTED
Red Gum Burl ■ 2013

6.5 x 5.5 x 5.5 cm
Australian red gum burl, tung oil, orange
oil; drilled, hand sanded, oiled
PHOTOGRAPHY BY ARTIST

PAULA BREYTER
Grandma's Curler ■ 2013
Bead: 4 x 1 x 3 cm
Sterling silver, silk raffia, thread; lost wax cast,
oxidized, soldered, hand fabricated
PHOTOGRAPHY BY ARTIST

CLAIRE MAUNSELL
Hollow Polymer Plank Beads ■ 2013
Each: 4 x 1 x 1 cm
Polymer clay, acrylic, ink; hollow
constructed, hand colored, sealed
PHOTOGRAPHY BY ARTIST

STEPHANIE WHITE
Beehive ▧ 2013
4 x 3 x 1.5 cm
Soft glass; flameworked, murrini, flat lapped, polished
PHOTOGRAPHY BY JEFFERY MARTINROE

MARY HARDING
Diary of Love ▧ 2012
1.9 x 1.9 x 0.5 cm
Hand-built earthenware
PHOTOGRAPHY BY ARTIST

SHANNON VICKERS
Burger ■ 2011
2.5 x 2.5 x 2.5 cm
Soda-lime glass; hand shaped,
flameworked, stringer application
PHOTOGRAPHY BY ARTIST

MARY HARDING
Carrots Down under ■ 2012
3.8 x 3.8 cm
Press-molded earthenware
PHOTOGRAPHY BY ARTIST

JANIE TRAINOR
Three Colorful Etched Beads with Spirals ■ 2012

Yellow bead: 1.5 x 0.6 cm
Red and green beads: 1.9 x 0.6 cm each
Soda-lime glass; flameworked, stringer
application, drawn, etched
PHOTOGRAPHY BY DAVID ORR

JONNA FAULKNER
Collaged Pod ▪ 2013

5.2 x 2.8 x 1.7 cm
Silver precious metal clay, cork clay
armature, 24-karat gold, pearls, liver of
sulfur patina; kiln fired, kum boo
PHOTOGRAPHY BY STEVE ROSSMAN

KIMBERLY NOGUEIRA
The Fool Who Lurks within Us ■ 2013

Wagon: 3.5 x 4 x 2.1 cm
Bronze, sterling and fine silver; fabricated, riveted
PHOTOGRAPHY BY WILLIAM STELZER

271

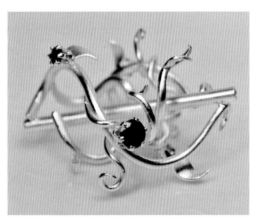

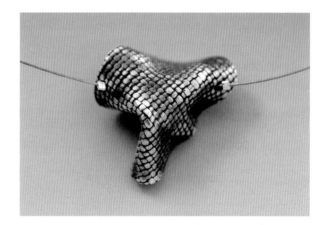

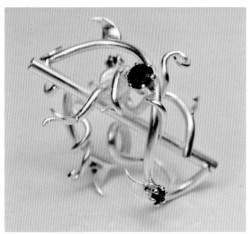

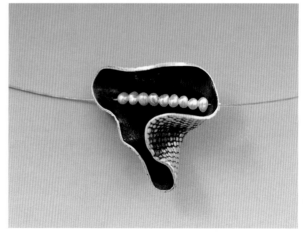

JULIE HENDRICKSON
Rose Garden Bead ■ 2013
2.5 x 1.8 x 1.8 cm
Sterling silver, rose garnet; fabricated

HOLLY KELLOGG
Drape/Front ■ 2012
10 x 12 x 5 cm
Metal clay, patina; textured

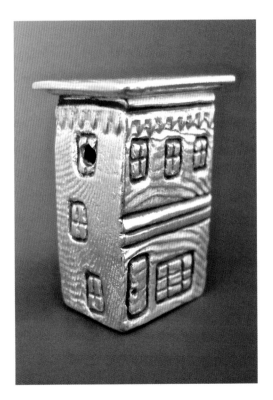

BETSY COLBY
Brownstone Bead ■ 2011
3.3 x 2 x 1.8 cm
Precious metal clay; handcrafted, kiln fired
PHOTOGRAPHY BY ARTIST

MONIKA URBANIAK
Untitled ■ 2013

Dimensions vary
Sterling silver, patina; hand fabricated,
depletion gilded, textured
PHOTOGRAPHY BY ARTIST

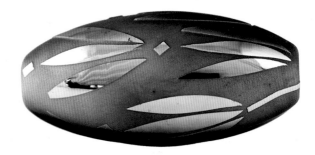

HOLLY COOPER
Copper Maza ■ 2013
4.5 x 2.1 cm
Glass; flameworked
PHOTOGRAPHY BY ARTIST

JEMMA CLEMENTS
Untitled ■ 2013
2.5 x 6 x 2.5 cm
Borosilicate glass, 24-karat gold;
handblown, sandblasted, fumed
PHOTOGRAPHY BY RICHARD CLEMENTS

MARTHA WILKES
Stacked Dots Over Encased Twistie—Round ■ 2013
2.5 x 3 x 3 cm
Soda-lime glass; flameworked
PHOTOGRAPHY BY JASON DOWDLE

EVE NAGODE
Spring Fever Spool Bead ■ 2013
6.4 x 3.2 x 3.2 cm
Glass, dagger beads, Czech drop beads;
flameworked, peyote stitch, whip stitch
PHOTOGRAPHY BY ARTIST

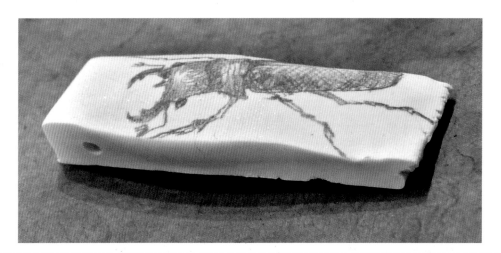

KELLY ROBERGE
Bug Beads ■ 2013

Each bead: 6.5 x 2 x 1 cm
Graphite transfer on polymer clay
PHOTOGRAPHY BY ARTIST

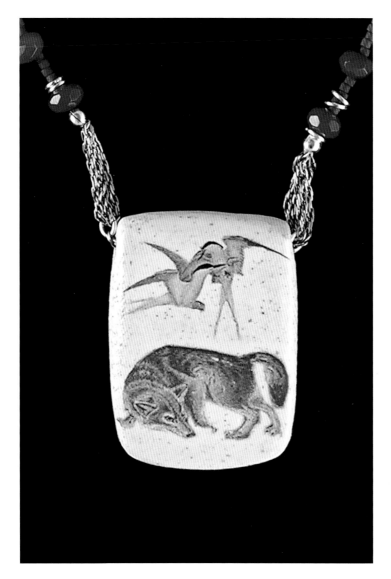

COURTNEY DICARLO
MARY ENGEL
Birds with Dog ■ 2011

3.5 x 2.5 x 0.8 cm
Ceramic with decal; handmade, glazed

SHU-LIN WU
Mokume-Gradient ■ 2011
4.9 x 32 x 32 cm
Porcelain, silver, steel wire; slip cast
PHOTOGRAPHY BY ARTIST

1000
beads

BEAU BARRETT
Cane Sphere ■ 2012
3.5 x 3.5 x 3.5 cm
Borosilicate glass; hollow blown
PHOTOGRAPHY BY ARTIST

DONNA PRUNKARD
Silver Blue Moon ■ 1213
4.6 x 4.6 x 4.6 cm
Borosilicate glass; hollow blown
PHOTOGRAPHY BY ARTIST

MELANIE MOERTEL
Monochrome Zoo ■ 2012

Each bead: 2.1 x 2.1 x 0.9 cm
Glass, sandstone; flameworked,
stringer application
PHOTOGRAPHY BY ARTIST

TOP
SANDRA BORNEMANN
Letter Bead ■ 2013

2.5 x 3.2 x 2.5 cm
Soda-lime glass, silver bead caps,
patina; flameworked, etched
PHOTOGRAPHY BY DIETER BORNEMANN

BOTTOM
ALI VANDEGRIFT
Ivory and Tuxedo Collection ■ 2013
Each: 3.2 x 3.2 x 3.2 cm
Glass, sterling silver; lampworked, capped, cored
PHOTOGRAPHY BY ARTIST

CARA HAYMAN
Hollow Black-and-White Flower Focal Bead ■ 2011
3 x 3.3 x 3.3 cm
Polymer clay; cane work, hand polished
PHOTOGRAPHY BY ARTIST

KATHERINE SPIGNESE
Five from the Black-and-White Series ■ 2011
Each bead: 2 x 1 x 0.8 cm
Polymer clay; cane work
PHOTOGRAPHY BY DOUG LEANY

SHANNON STEELE
My Pretty Pods ■ 2013

Each: 1.9 x 1.9 x 1.9 cm
Soda-lime glass; flameworked
PHOTOGRAPHY BY SALLY STEVENS

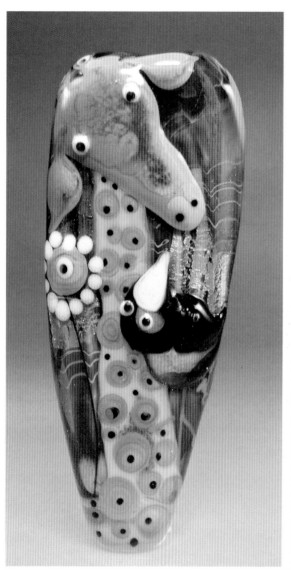

MANUELA WUTSCHKE
Esmeralda ▨ 2013
7.5 x 2.8 x 1.2 cm
Soda-lime glass, silver foil, enamels;
flameworked, stringer work, encased
PHOTOGRAPHY BY ARTIST

LOUISE LITTLE
Oro Valley ■ 2012
3.2 x 4.4 x 3.2 cm
Soda-lime glass, bronze and silver bead caps;
hollow blown, lampworked, etched, riveted
PHOTOGRAPHY BY DAVID ORR

YVONNE VILLENEUVE
Lava Flow ■ 2012
2.5 x 3.8 x 2.5 cm
Vitreous enamel, copper; kiln fired
PHOTOGRAPHY BY ARTIST

AMY LEMAIRE
Emergence Bead Pair ▪ 2013

Left: 2 x 2.5 x 1.5 cm; right: 2.5 x 2 x 1.2 cm
Soda-lime glass; flameworked,
cold worked
PHOTOGRAPHY BY ARTIST

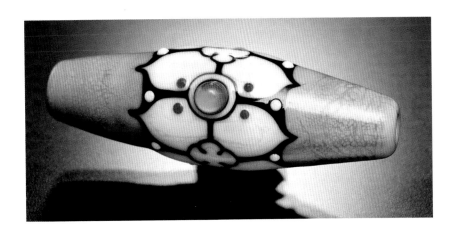

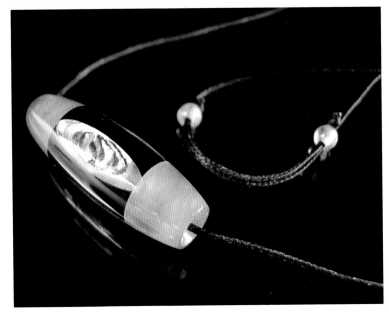

TERRI CASPARY SCHMIDT
Green Church Window Bicone ▨ 2013

4.6 x 1.8 x 1.8 cm
Soda-lime glass; lampworked

ALLAN SPEHAR
All-California Duplex Bead ▨ 2012

4.1 x 1.8 x 1.8 cm
Red abalone from California, black jade from
the Sierra Nevada foothills, honey garnet from
Happy Camp, California; hand worked

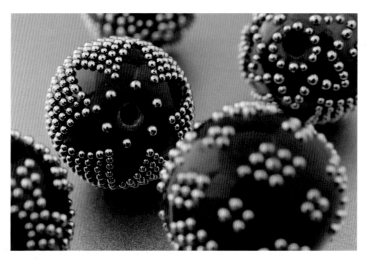

ANNE-LISE MEIER
Dot by Dot ■ 2013
Each: 2.1 x 2.1 x·2.1 cm
Glass, luster; flameworked
PHOTOGRAPHY BY ARTIST

AURELIO CASTANO
Ribbon Beads ■ 2013

Left: 2.5 x 2.5 x 2.5 cm; right: 0.6 x 0.6 x 2.5 cm
Recycled ribbon, recycled wooden beads, recycled
plastic rolls from register tape; basketry
PHOTOGRAPHY BY ARTIST

MARCY SWANSON
Sisters Beads ■ 2013

Left: 5.5 x 4.5 2.5 cm; center: 1.3 x 2.5 x 1.5 cm; right: 3 x 6.5 x 2 cm
Antique tintypes and tobacco tins, patina, copper, brass
rivets and tubes; hydraulic pressed, cold constructed
PHOTOGRAPHY BY GERRIT KELLY

1000
beads

MELANIE ROWE
Geometric Transformation ■ 2012

Left: 3 cm high; center: 2.5 cm high; right: 5 cm wide
Silver clay, patina
PHOTOGRAPHY BY SUSAN EWART

JANET GRAFF
Gears Around ■ 2012

Dimensions vary
Found objects, bead caps; cold formed, riveted
PHOTOGRAPHY BY NATHANIEL GRAFF

JASON MORRISSEY
Secret Language of Birthdays Bead ■ 2007

4.5 x 2. cm
Copper, 18-karat red gold, sterling silver;
etched, tube riveted, cold connected

293

TAMARA GRÜNER
Diminovula ■ 2011
2.4 x 1.8 x 1.8 cm
Porcelain; cast, mounted
PHOTOGRAPHY BY ARTIST

NATALIE PAPPAS
Crackled White Ceramic Bead ■ 2012
0.8 x 0.8 x 0.8 cm
Porcelain, glaze, rhinestone crystals;
hand formed, fired, cone 1
PHOTOGRAPHY BY ARTIST

KAREN BACHMANN
Burnt Sphere Necklace ■ 2011

4 x 50 x 4 cm
Maple wood, onyx, sterling silver;
lathe turned, pyrography, strung
PHOTOGRAPHY BY RALPH GABRINER

KAY BONITZ
Bead with Button Pearl ■ 2013

2.5 x 1.2 x 0.5 cm
Polymer clay, inlaid button pearl, mokume
gane; die formed, image transfer
PHOTOGRAPHY BY WERNER BONITZ

ANN LUMSDEN
Vacation ■ 2013

Each bead: 1.5 x 3.3 x 3.3 cm
Glass and aluminum watch cases,
vintage postcards; assembled
PHOTOGRAPHY BY ARTIST

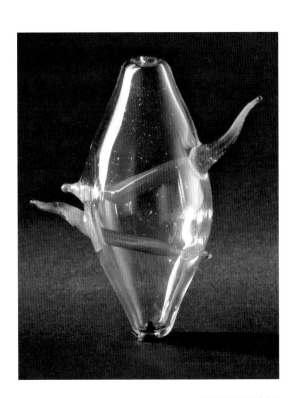

SALLY PRASCH
Passing Through ■ 2013
1.5 x 1 x 1 cm
Borosilicate, glass; flameworked
PHOTOGRAPHY BY MIKE BRANDT

COURTNEY DICARLO
MARY ENGEL
Fox and Hound ■ 2011
2 x 4.5 x 0.8 cm
Ceramic with decal; handmade, glazed
PHOTOGRAPHY BY ARTISTS

SHELBY FITZPATRICK
Fishing ▪ 2012
20 x 20 x 2 cm
Silver, jasper, mokume gane; fused, fabricated
PHOTOGRAPHY BY MIKE BLISSETT

SASHA CASE
Gypsy Bead ■ 2013
3.8 x 2 x 2 cm
Silver precious metal clay, bisque bead, sterling silver chain,
cubic zirconias; painted, embellished, syringe technique
PHOTOGRAPHY BY ARTIST

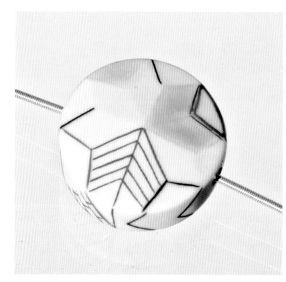

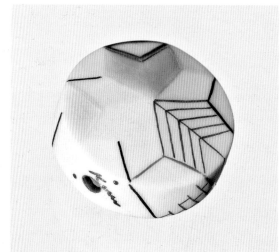

PATTI CAHILL
Summer of Love Dancing Flower Bead ■ 2012
1.5 x 2 x 2 cm
Blown glass; dotted, raked, masked, plucked, twisted
PHOTOGRAPHY BY ARTIST

KAREN MASSARO
Reversible Bead ■ 2013
1.2 x 2.5 cm
Slip-cast porcelain, glaze, gold luster
PHOTOGRAPHY BY ARTIST

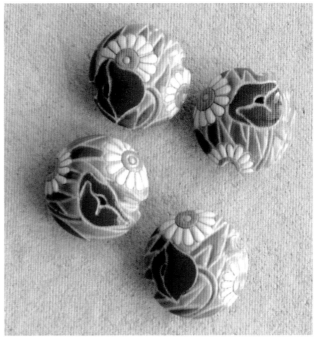

MARTHA WILKES
*Stacked Dots over Encased
Twistie—Bicone* ■ 2013

3 x 3.2 x 3.2 cm
Soda-lime glass; encased, flameworked
PHOTOGRAPHY BY JASON DOWDLE

VLADISLAV IVANOV
Summer Meadow ■ 2012

Each: 1.1 x 2.3 x 2.3 cm
Stoneware clay, glazes; bisque, cone
5, hand carved and painted
PHOTOGRAPHY BY ARTIST

WIWAT KAMOLPORNWIJIT
Spiral ■ 2010

4 x 50 x 4 cm
Polymer clay; hand formed, layered, rolled
PHOTOGRAPHY BY ARTIST

SO YOUNG PARK
From the Fall ▦ 2012

7 x 5 x 1.5 cm
Silver, 24-karat gold leaf, garnet, peridot, smoky
quartz; oxidized, hammered, soldered, beaded
PHOTOGRAPHY BY MUNCH STUDIO

DEDE LEUPOLD
Spring Thing Bead ■ 2013
3.5 x 3.5 x 0.8 cm
Polymer clay, sterling silver; millefiori
PHOTOGRAPHY BY ARTIST

JANICE PEACOCK
Aurora Necklace ■ 2011

Center bead: 5 x 3 cm
Soda-lime glass, silver foil; flameworked
PHOTOGRAPHY BY AZAD

ANNE MORGAN
Lava Twist Necklace with Garnet ■ 2011

20 x 20 x 2.5 cm
Silver, garnet, lava, silver spacers; reticulated,
fabricated, soldered, stone setting
PHOTOGRAPHY BY SIMON CHAPMAN

VICKI SCHNEIDER
Casey ■ 2013
3.2 x 3.2 x 2.5 cm
Soda-lime glass; flameworked
PHOTOGRAPHY BY ARTIST

SUSAN MATYCH-HAGER
Mr. Chickadee ■ 2013
40 x 50 x 25 cm
Soda-lime glass; flameworked, sculpted, etched
PHOTOGRAPHY BY ARTIST

DIANE VILLANO
Big Bead—Kiffa Bead ■ 2013
20.3 x 12.7 x 7 cm
Polymer clay, papier-mâché; kumihimo braiding
PHOTOGRAPHY BY ELIZABETH MILLS

CARA HAYMAN
Thumbprints in Richness Focal Bead ■ 2013
8.6 x 3.3 x 1.4 cm
Polymer clay, gold leaf; hand crafted, cane work
PHOTOGRAPHY BY ARTIST

JODY LEE
Monochrome Garden ■ 2012
2.5 x 3 x 0.8 cm
Soda-lime glass; flameworked

BRONDWYN VIVIAN
Ivory Discs ■ 2012
Dimensions vary
Soda-lime glass; flameworked, shaped,
annealed, cold worked

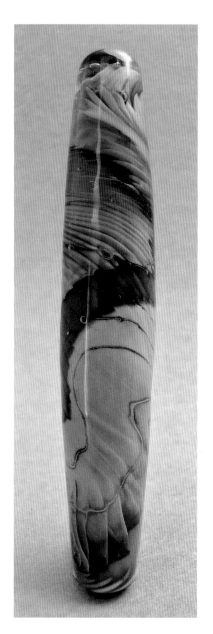

IVY BOYER
Cosmic Swirl ■ 2012
1.7 x 0.5 x 0.8 cm
Effetre glass, ivory base bead; lampworked
PHOTOGRAPHY BY DAVID ORR

JANIE MATTHEWS
Storm at Sunset ■ 2012
7 x 1.3 x 1.3 cm
Soft glass; flameworked
PHOTOGRAPHY BY ARTIST

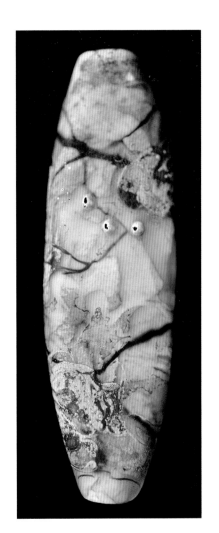

W. BRAD PEARSON
Lotus Series Bead ■ 2012

3.9 x 2.1 x 2.1 cm
Glass; flameworked
PHOTOGRAPHY BY ARTIST

JOHN WINTER
Blue Hole ■ 2012

0.6 x 2.4 x 0.5 cm
Soda-lime glass, silver leaf,
silver wire; flameworked
PHOTOGRAPHY BY JOHN WINTER

JONNA FAULKNER
Night Flight ■ 2013
6.2 x 1.7 x 0.7 cm
Silver precious metal clay, cork clay armature, 24-karat
gold, liver-of-sulfur patina; kiln fired, kum boo
PHOTOGRAPHY BY STEVE ROSSMAN

DOROTHY MCMILLAN
Screened Lentils ■ 2012
Each: 1 x 1 x 1 cm
Polymer clay; silk-screened
PHOTOGRAPHY BY ARTIST

TOVE EGHOLT
Koi ■ 2010
4 x 7 x 3 cm
Glass; flameworked
PHOTOGRAPHY BY DAVID BICHO

MARGARET ZINSER
Hungry Caterpillar ■ 2012
1.5 x 1.5 x 0.5 cm
Glass, vitreous enamel; flameworked, hand painted
PHOTOGRAPHY BY ARTIST

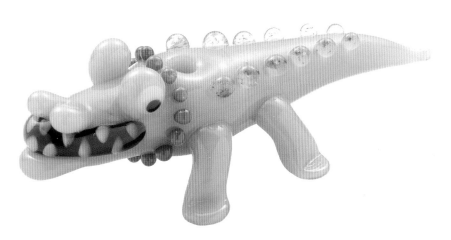

STEPHANIE SERSICH
Lucretia ■ 2013

1.8 x 6 x 2.5 cm
Glass; lampworked
PHOTOGRAPHY BY TOM EICHLER

JOSEAN GARCIA
Multicolor ■ 2013

Largest bead: 1.5 x 2.1 x 5.5 cm
Blown glass; roll-up technique
PHOTOGRAPHY BY ARTIST

BETH MILLNER
Four Seasons Pillow Bead Necklace ■ 2013

Each bead: 1.2 x 1.2 x 0.5 cm
Sterling silver sheet and wire; hand fabricated, sawn, formed,
soldered, stamped, oxidized, woven, tumbled, brushed
PHOTOGRAPHY BY CHRISTY BUDNICK

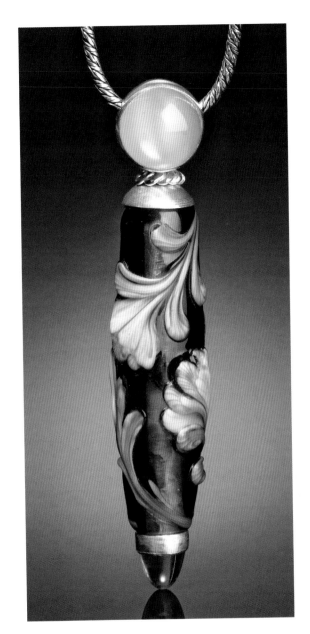

KRISTEN FRANTZEN ORR
Blossoms under a Peach Moon ▪ 2012

7.6 x 2 x 2 cm

Soda-lime glass, sterling silver, peach moonstone, cabachon,
quartz bullet; flameworked, cane decoration, chemically etched

METALWORK BY GAIL RAPPA
PHOTOGRAPHY BY DAVID ORR

JODY LEE
Monochrome Garden ▪ 2012

2.5 x 3 x 0.8 cm
Soda-lime glass; flameworked
PHOTOGRAPHY BY ARTIST

PHYLLIS DINTENFASS
Puffums Array ■ 2010

Each: 1 x 2 x 1 cm
Glass seed beads; peyote stitch
PHOTOGRAPHY BY MARK DINTENFASS

TOP
ELENA MIKLUSH
Focus Bead ▧ 2013

3 x 4.5 x 4.5 cm
Seed beads, nylon thread; micro-macramé
PHOTOGRAPHY BY ARTIST

BOTTOM
LILY LIU
YB1 ▧ 2013

Largest: 6.5 x 1.3 x 1.3 cm
Seed beads, glass beads, cotton
and wool yarn; knitted
PHOTOGRAPHY BY THE ARTIST

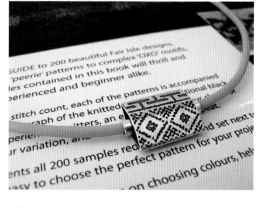

NORIKAZU KOGURE
Tonbodama Bead ▓ 2011
2.5 x 2.2 x 2.2 cm
Glass; flameworked
PHOTOGRAPHY BY ARTIST

KIRSTY MUIR
Etched Fair Isle Bead ▓ 2013
2 x 1.7 x 0.5 cm
Sterling silver; etched, formed, oxidized
PHOTOGRAPHY BY ARTIST

AMY WALDMAN-SMITH
Selection of Ottoman/Bakbuk Beads ■ 2012

Largest bead: 5 x 1.8 x 1.8 cm
Soda-lime glass; lampworked, masked, raked
PHOTOGRAPHY BY ANN CADY

COLLEEN WHITE
Three Bronze Metal Clay Beads ■ 2013
Left: 3.4 x 3.3 x 1.2 cm
Center: 2.3 x 2.6 x 2 cm
Right: 3 x 1.8 x 1.2 cm
Glass, bronze metal clay, cubic zirconias; hand built
PHOTOGRAPHY BY ARTIST

PAULA MCDOWELL
Box and Tiki Man Beads ▥ 2011

Left: 2.5 x 2.5 x 1.2 cm; right: 5 x 1.2 x 28 cm
Silver precious metal clay, fine silver; hand
built, kiln fired, mitered, oxidized, polished
PHOTOGRAPHY BY BRAD MOON

JULIE BLANKENSHIP
Southwestern Sculpted Pot Beads ■ 2012

Dimensions vary
Polymer clay; hand sculpted and finished
PHOTOGRAPHY BY ARTIST

BONNIE POLINSKI
Myopic Sentinal ■ 2012

2.8 x 2.8 x 1.5 cm
Clay, sterling silver wire, Swarovski crystal,
glaze, brass prong settings; raku fired,
soldered, silversmithing techniques
PHOTOGRAPHY BY ARTIST

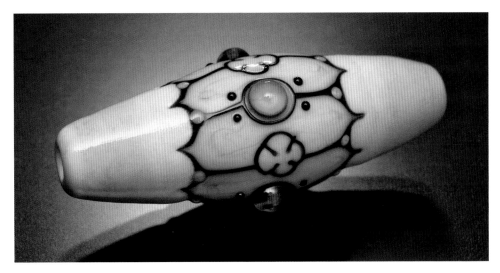

NORIKAZU KOGURE
Tonbodama Bead ■ 2011

2.5 x 2.2 x 2.2 cm
Glass; flameworked
PHOTOGRAPHY BY ARTIST

TERRI CASPARY SCHMIDT
Blue-and-Ivory Church Window Bicone ■ 2013

4.6 x 1.9 x 1.9 cm
Soda-lime glass; lampworked
PHOTOGRAPHY BY MARGOT GEIST

325

BEAU BARRETT
Laminar Capsules ■ 2012

Each: 5 x 2.5 x 2.5 cm
Borosilicate glass; hollow blown
PHOTOGRAPHY BY ARTIST

KAREN LEWIS
Veneer Art Beads ■ 2012

4 x 3 x 1 cm
Polymer clay; multilayered cane
work, collage technique
PHOTOGRAPHY BY WAYNE ROBBINS

327

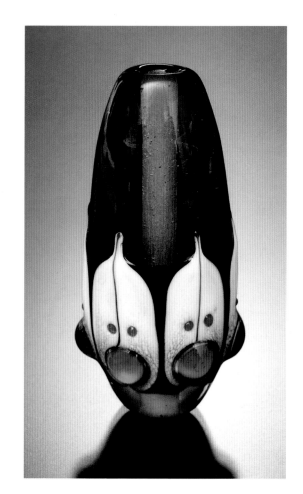

DAYLE DOROSHOW
Planets Bead ■ 2012
1.5 x 1 x 1 cm
Polymer clay; millefiori, collaged, textured
PHOTOGRAPHY BY ARTIST

TERRI CASPARY SCHMIDT
Leaf Study No. 1 ■ 2013
4.2 x 2 x 2 cm
Soda-lime glass; lampworked
PHOTOGRAPHY BY MARGOT GEIST

RONIT DAGAN
*From the Mystery of the Turning Beads
Series: Self-Portrait* ■ 2012
20 x 7 x 7 cm
Borosilicate glass, oil paint; flameworked,
sandblasted, coldworked
PHOTOGRAPHY BY LEV NISSIM

JENN ZITKOV
Sea Fossil ■ 2013
3.8 x 2 cm
Glass, enamel; flameworked
PHOTOGRAPHY BY ARTIST

SO YOUNG PARK
Oriental Hill I ■ 2010
15 x 15 x 1.5 cm
Silver, 24-karat yellow gold leaf, freshwater pearls; oxidized,
hand fabricated, hammered, soldered, hand engraved
PHOTOGRAPHY BY ARTIST

CYNTHIA GAVIÃO
Acaso ■ 2013
2 x 1.5 x 1 cm
Porcelain, paper clay; fired, cone 9
PHOTOGRAPHY BY PAULO SILVA

MELISSA GRAKOWSKY SHIPPEE
Sunken Treasure Pendants ■ 2013

Each: 2.5 x 2.5 x 1 cm
Bottle caps, sand, shells, pearls, crystal, resin,
aluminum tubing; drilled, hammered
PHOTOGRAPHY BY ARTIST

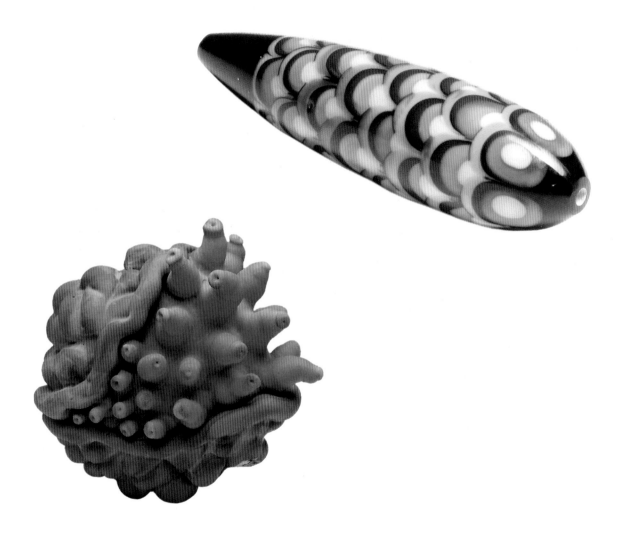

AMY LEMAIRE
Emergence Bead ■ 2013
3 x 2.5 x 1.5 cm
Soda-lime glass; flameworked, cold worked
PHOTOGRAPHY BY ARTIST

MATHIEU GRODET
Colored Scale ■ 2012
4.9 x 1.3 x 1.3 cm
Glass; flameworked
PHOTOGRAPHY BY TANYA LYONS

1000
beads

MANUELA WUTSCHKE
Spirit of Love ■ 2013
6.3 x 2.8 x 1.3 cm
Soda-lime glass, cubic zirconia, goldstone,
enamel; flameworked, stringer work, encased

PATTY LAKINSMITH
Reptilian Series ■ 2011

Left: 4 x 3 x 1 cm; center: 4 x 2 cm; right: 3.7 x 3 x 1 cm
Soda-lime glass; flameworked
PHOTOGRAPHY BY DAVID ORR

SHELBY FITZPATRICK
Landscaping ■ 2012
20 x 20 x 2 cm
Silver, jasper beads, mokume gane; fused, fabricated
PHOTOGRAPHY BY MIKE BLISSETT

SHERRY BELLAMY
Dancer ■ 2011
1.2 x 1.2 x 0.8 cm
Glass; flameworked, imploded
PHOTOGRAPHY BY ARTIST

DAWN LOMBARD
Stone ■ 2013
5 x 2.5 x 0.8 cm
Glass, silver leaf, silvered ivory, fine
silver wire; flameworked
PHOTOGRAPHY BY PATRICK MANNING

NORIKAZU KOGURE
Tonbodama Bead ■ 2012

3.5 x 2.8 x 2.8 cm
Glass; flameworked
PHOTOGRAPHY BY ARTIST

NANCY WORDEN
Double IBM Ball Bead ■ 2012

5 x 3.3 x 3.3 cm
Typewriter balls, tax tokens, copper, gold
leaf, patina; fabricated, electroformed
PHOTOGRAPHY BY REX RYSTEDT

FLORIANE LATAILLE
Tricot ■ 2011

Each: 5 x 5 x 5 cm
Soft glass; flameworked
PHOTOGRAPHY BY ARTIST

ANGELA MARTIN KOBRICK
Majolica Knot Beads ■ 2012

Each: 1.7 cm in diameter
Hand-built terra cotta; electric fired, cone
04, majolica glazed and painted, cone 06
PHOTOGRAPHY BY THOMAS J. KOBRICK

HEATHER TRIMLETT
Anaheim Disks Stacked ■ 2012
Largest: 5.5 x .75 cm
Soda-lime glass; flameworked, layered with
twists and cased stringer, polished
PHOTOGRAPHY BY DAVID ORR

MARTHA WILKES
Knotted Necklace of Dotted Beads ■ 2011

46 x 1.8 x 1.8 cm
Soda-lime glass; flameworked
PHOTOGRAPHY BY JASON DOWDLE

TOP
NATHALIE LECLAIR
Growing ■ 2012

Largest bead: 2 x 4.4 x 4.4 cm
Soda-lime glass; flameworked, molded
PHOTOGRAPHY BY PATRICK ROGER

BOTTOM
MICHAELA MARIA MOELLER
Untitled ■ 2010

3 x 3 x 45 cm
Glass, silver bead caps, custom-made rubber;
flameworked, engraved, fire polished
PHOTOGRAPHY BY ARTIST

LISA-JANE HARVEY
Flame Lily Transient Treasure ■ 2010
6 x 6 x 1.5 cm
Soda-lime glass, sterling silver; flameworked
PHOTOGRAPHY BY BIRGIT UTECH

PATRICK DUGGAN
Glamour Spikes ■ 2012
4.1 x 3 x 3 cm
Seed beads, Czech drops; netting, peyote stitch
PHOTOGRAPHY BY NEVA BROWN

TOP
LORETTA TRYON
Nefertiti Bead ■ 2012

2.5 x 8 x 2.5 cm
Bronze, sterling, silver, patina;
synclastic formed, engraved
PHOTOGRAPHY BY MICHAEL T. PYLE

BOTTOM
ALI VANDEGRIFT
Ivory and Copper Green Bicone ■ 2013

11.8 x 2.7 x 2.7 cm
Glass; lampworked, etched, capped
PHOTOGRAPHY BY ARTIST

LISA KLAKULAK
Accordion Bead Form Study ■ 2013

17.8 x 17.8 x 3.8 cm
Wool fiber, cotton thread; wet felted, sculpted,
free-motion machine stitched/embossed
PHOTOGRAPHY BY MARY VOGEL

345

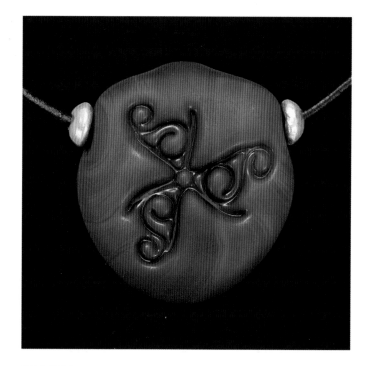

KYLIE PARRY
Red Barn ■ 2013
2 x 1.8 x 0.9 cm
Hand-formed and carved
stoneware; glazed
PHOTOGRAPHY BY ARTIST

GILA FOX
Triberst ■ 2012
3.4 x 3.4 x 0.9 cm
Soda-lime glass, handmade stamp; flameworked, etched
PHOTOGRAPHY BY TIM FOX

LENKA ŠVÁCHOVÁ
Stone ■ 2012

Long beads: 1.4 x 1.5 x 1.5 cm each
Round beads: 1.4 x 1.5 x 1.5 cm each
Polymer clay
PHOTOGRAPHY BY ARTIST

CLAIRE MAUNSELL
Marbled Hollow Box Strata Bead ■ 2013

2.3 x 2.3 x 2.3 cm
Polymer clay; hollow constructed,
manipulated, colored, distressed
PHOTOGRAPHY BY ARTIST

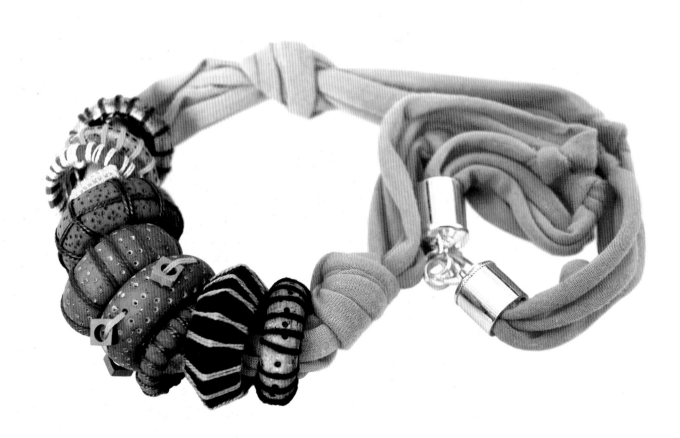

IRIS MISHLY
Life-Savers Beads ■ 2012
Each bead: 5 x 2 x 2 cm
Polymer clay, embroidery thread; extruded
PHOTOGRAPHY BY ARTIST

LORETTA LAM
New Berry Cluster ■ 2012

10 x 46 x 1.8 cm
Polymer beads, sterling silver cable;
hollow formed, millefiori, Skinner blend
PHOTOGRAPHY BY DOUG YAPLE

LUDMILA SIKOLOVÁ
Homage to Glass Beads ■ 2011
32 x 32 x 9 cm
Polyester, digital print
PHOTOGRAPHY BY ARTIST

LUDMILA SIKOLOVÁ
Homage to Glass Beads ■ 2011
25 x 25 x 5 cm
Polyester, steel wire, digital print
PHOTOGRAPHY BY ARTIST

ISABELLA PIKART
Cubo Family ■ 2012

Dimensions vary
Porcelain; gold plated
PHOTOGRAPHY BY JULIA KRÜGER

VLADISLAV IVANOV
Pink Sunrise ■ 2012
Each: 0.9 x 1.8 x 1.8 cm
Stoneware clay, glazes; bisque,
cone 5, hand carved and painted
PHOTOGRAPHY BY ARTIST

NATALIE PAPPAS
*Lavender Nugget with Flower
Texture Ceramic Bead* ■ 2012

1 x 0.5 x 0.5 cm
Porcelain clay, underglaze, overglaze;
hand formed, textured, fired, cone 1
PHOTOGRAPHY BY ARTIST

LOUISE LITTLE
Painted Desert ■ 2012

43.2 x 5.1 x 2.5 cm
Glass, brass, bronze and silver bead caps; hollow
blown, lampworked, tube riveted, etched, beaded
PHOTOGRAPHY BY DAVID ORR

ABIGAIL YOUDIM
Pop up ■ 2012
5 x 20 x 20 cm
Polymer pigments, silver; cast, threaded
PHOTOGRAPHY BY EMILY NHAISSI

HOLLY COOPER
Rara Avis ▓ 2013

5.5 x 1.7 cm
Glass; flameworked
PHOTOGRAPHY BY ARTIST

MARADA GENZ
Sunflower ■ 2013

Overall length: 45 cm
Polymer clay; formed, cured,
drilled, sanded, strung
PHOTOGRAPHY BY ARTIST

KAY BONITZ
Brain Cane Lentils ■ 2013

Each bead: 1.2 x 1.2 x 0.2 cm
Polymer clay; millefiori cane technique
PHOTOGRAPHY BY WERNER BONITZ

HEATHER BEHRENDT
Silver on Ivory ▪ 2013

Each bead: 0.7 x 1.7 x 1.7 cm
Soda-lime glass; flameworked, pressed
PHOTOGRAPHY BY ARTIST

LAUREN BUTLER
Prima Donna ■ 2012
8.5 x 1.5 x 38 cm
Old sheet music, Swarovski pearls and crystal
pearls, natural smoky quartz; cut, rolled,
glued, sealed, strung, right-angle weave

HOLLY COOPER
Thera ■ 2013

5.7 x 2.6 cm
Glass; flameworked
PHOTOGRAPHY BY ARTIST

TAMARA GRÜNER
Kein Stern von Oben ■ 2013
9 x 2.5 x 2.5 cm
Porcelain; cast, carved, milled

MICHAELA MARIA MOELLER
Untitled ■ 2011

3 x 3 x 45 cm
Glass, gold plate, custom-made
rubber; flameworked, engraved
PHOTOGRAPHY BY ARTIST

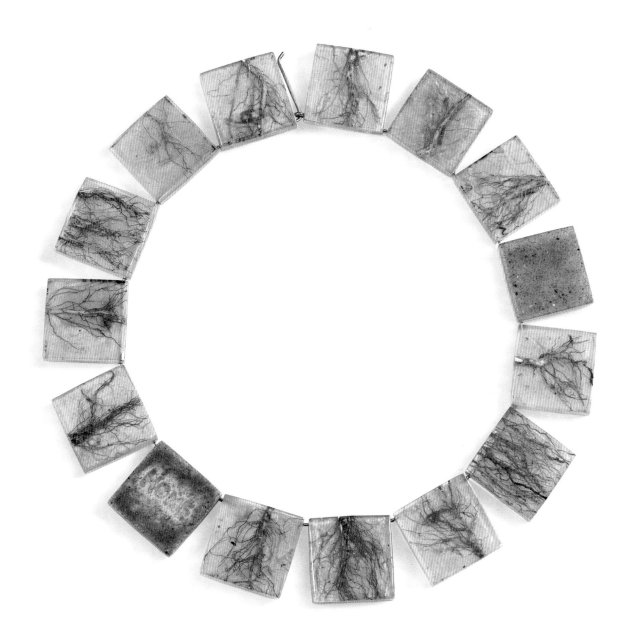

DANIA CHELMINSKY
DecoRoots Necklace ■ 2012

Overall length: 22 x 22 x 0.6 cm; each bead: 3 x 3 x 0.6 cm
Roots, handmade paper, epoxy, gold; hand fabricated, cast
PHOTOGRAPHY BY RAN ERDE

CAROL BLACKBURN
Tetra Beads ▥ 2012

Largest bead: 5.1 x 5.1 cm
Polymer clay, wooden beads
PHOTOGRAPHY BY ARTIST

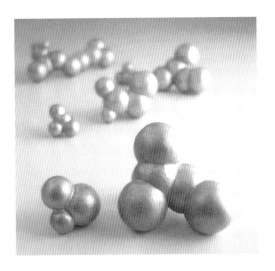

TOVE KNUTS

Molluscamolecule Earrings ■ 2012

Largest: 3 x 2 x 1.5 cm
Wooden beads, silver, mother-of-
pearl; ground, painted
PHOTOGRAPHY BY ARTIST

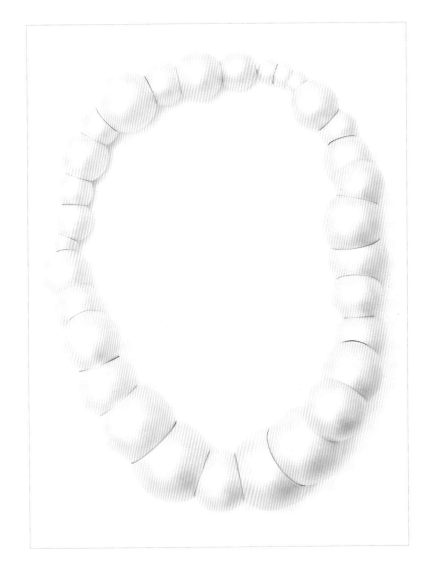

TOVE KNUTS

Molluscamolecule Necklace ■ 2011

45 x 5 x 5 cm
Wooden beads, silver; ground, painted
PHOTOGRAPHY BY ARTIST

BARBARA SIMON
Mom and Apple Pie Beads ■ 2012
Largest bead: 5.5 x 3 x 1.5 cm
Soft glass, gilder's paste; sandblasted
PHOTOGRAPHY BY BABETTE BELMONDO

ANN KLEM
Faceted Cubes ■ 2013
Each bead: 0.5 x 0.5 x 0.5 cm
Sheet glass; kiln formed, fused, cut, polished, cold worked
PHOTOGRAPHY BY GEOFF CARR

LIBBY LEUCHTMAN
Carved Bead ■ 2012
4 x 2.5 x 2.5 cm
Glass; flameworked, carved, cold worked
PHOTOGRAPHY BY ARTIST

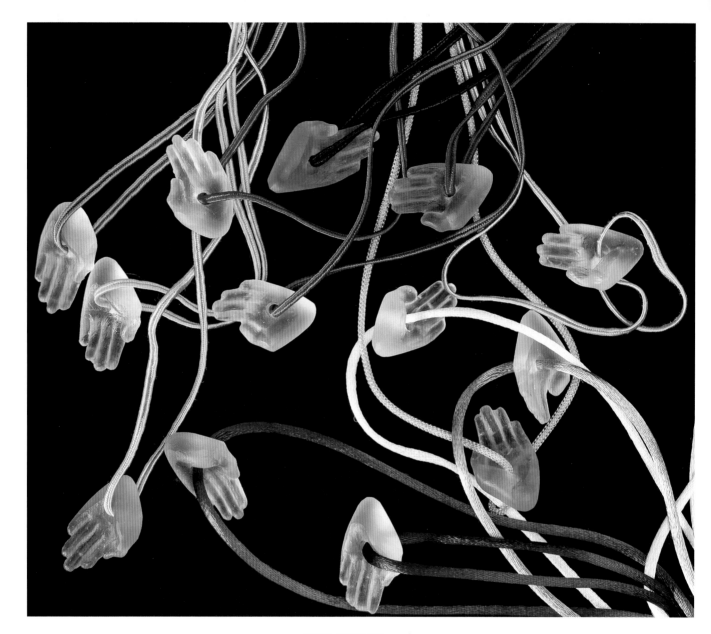

ANNA BOOTHE

Give 'Em a Hand ▨ 2012

Each bead: 3 x 1.9 x 1.2 cm
Lead crystal; kiln cast
PHOTOGRAPHY BY RICK ECHELMEYER

HEATHER TRIMLETT
Standing Anaheim Disks ■ 2012

Largest: 5.5 x .75 cm
Soda-lime glass; flameworked, layered
with twists and cased stringer, polished

CARLA DI FRANCESCO
Mic Mac Beads ■ 2013

Dimensions vary
Soft glass; lampworked
PHOTOGRAPHY BY ARTIST

LISA LISCHKA
Tide Pool ▪ 2013

4 x 1.8 x 0.8 cm
Sheet glass; fused, cold worked

JOSEAN GARCIA
Blue Beads ▪ 2013

Largest bead: 4 cm in diameter
Blown glass; roll-up technique

ANGELA MEIER
Wheel of Fortune ■ 2012
4 x 4 x 1.1 cm
Soda-lime glass, silver precious metal
clay, sterling silver; flameworked
PHOTOGRAPHY BY ARTIST

FLORIANE LATAILLE
Arc en Ciel ■ 2012
15 x 15 x 2 cm
Soft glass, silver; flameworked
PHOTOGRAPHY BY ARTIST

LISA FLETCHER
Nautilus ▓ 2012
3.8 x 2 x 1.3 cm
Soda-lime glass; flameworked,
layered, encased, pressed
PHOTOGRAPHY BY ARTIST

DARCY YORK
Clio Tides ▓ 2012
3 x 3 x 1.4 cm
Soda-lime glass, silver glass; flameworked
PHOTOGRAPHY BY ARTIST

ANITA SPENCER
Pink Miró ■ 2013
3.1 x 3.4 x 2 cm
Soda-lime glass, powdered glass enamels;
flameworked, applied murrini

PENNY DICKINSON
Twisted Window Bead ■ 2012
3 x 0.8 x 0.8 cm
Soda-lime glass, silver glass; flameworked

ALI VANDEGRIFT
Purple and Copper Green Bicone ■ 2013
11.7 x 3.3 x 3.3 cm
Glass; lampworked, etched
PHOTOGRAPHY BY ARTIST

ERIKA FERRARIN
From the Fiore:Lini Series: Disco D'oro ■ 2012

7 x 5 x 2.5 cm
Earthenware clay, rubber tubing, glass, shell, silver
findings, wooden disk; electric fired, underglazed,
flamed, assembled, threaded, hand textured and painted
PHOTOGRAPHY BY LEN WARD

LESLIE KAPLAN
Summer ■ 2012

Largest bead: 1.3 cm in diameter
Glass; flameworked
PHOTOGRAPHY BY LARRY BERMAN

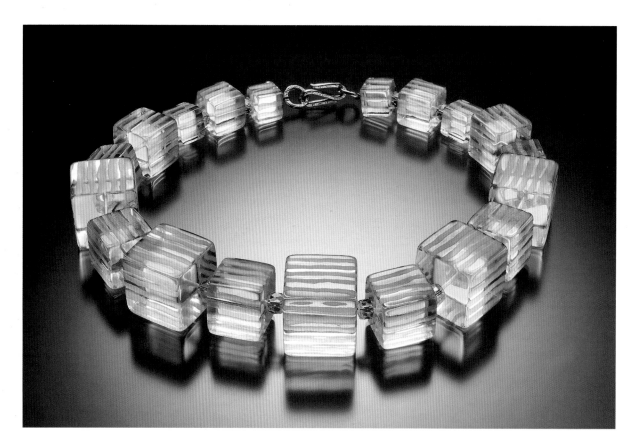

KAREN BACHMANN
Ice Cube Necklace ■ 2011

3.8 x 3.8 x 47.7 cm
Acrylic resin, rock crystal, sterling
silver; carved, polished, cast, strung
PHOTOGRAPHY BY RALPH GABRINER

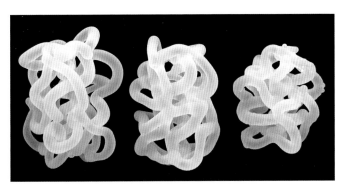

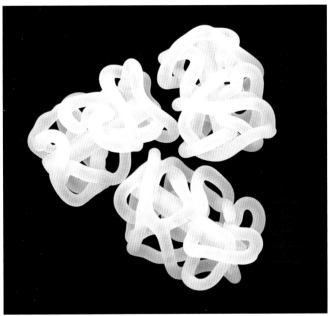

VANESSA HAHN
Fusilli in Glass x 3 ■ 2011
40 x 35 x 20 cm
Borosilicate glass; flameworked, sandblasted
PHOTOGRAPHY BY ARTIST

SOGANG JEON
Fruit ■ 2013
44 x 21 x 5 cm
Plastic straw, silver plating, brass, resin; melted, cast
PHOTOGRAPHY BY MUNCH STUDIO

AMANDA MUDDIMER
Roses and Castles ▪ 2013

Each bead: 1.5 x 1.5 x 1.5 cm
Soda-lime glass; flameworked
PHOTOGRAPHY BY PENNY OLIVER

ANN KLEM
Cubes, of Course! ▪ 2013

Each bead: 0.6 x 0.6 x 0.6 cm
Sheet glass; kiln formed, fused, cut, ground,
tumbled, polished cold worked
PHOTOGRAPHY BY GEOFF CARR

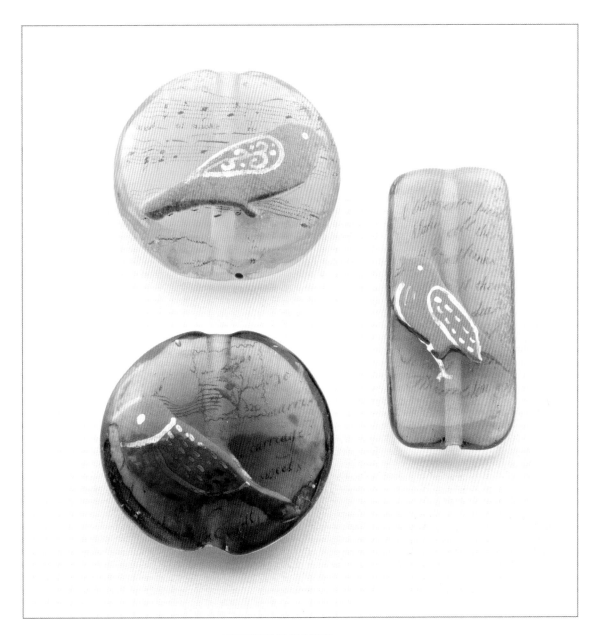

BECKY FAIRCLOUGH
Tweets ■ 2011

Round beads: 2.8 x 3 x 1.1 cm each
Long bead: 3.8 x 1.4 x 0.6 cm
Soda-lime glass, enamel transfers,
lusters; flameworked
PHOTOGRAPHY BY ARTIST

HEATHER SELLERS
Rainbow Swirls ■ 2013
1.5 x 9 x 1.5 cm
Glass; flameworked, encased
PHOTOGRAPHY BY ARTIST

AMBER BALLARD
Rainbow Bubbles Bead ■ 2012
4.4 x 3.2 x 0.6 cm
Glass; flameworked
PHOTOGRAPHY BY ARTIST

1000
beads

BARBARA PAZ
Primo Necklace ■ 2012
25 x 25 x 2 cm
Bombyx mori silkworm cocoon,
sterling silver; constructed
PHOTOGRAPHY BY DAMIAN WASSER

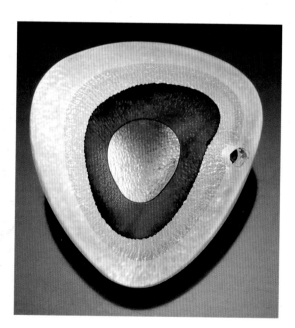

DOLORES BARRETT
Silver Triangle Bead ■ 2011
2 x 1.7 x 0.7 cm
Glass, silver foil; fused, slumped, carved
PHOTOGRAPHY BY ARTIST

KAY BONITZ
Bead with Cornflake Pearl ■ 2013
1.2 x 1.5 x 0.7 cm
Polymer clay, inlaid pearl, mokume
gane; die formed, image transfer
PHOTOGRAPHY BY WERNER BONITZ

NANCY SCHINDLER
Life Tangle ■ 2011

Each: 5.1 x 5.1 cm
Porcelain; hand built, hand carved
PHOTOGRAPHY BY ARTIST

JEN ZITKOV
Wave ■ 2013
3.8 x 2.5 cm
Glass, enamel; flameworked
PHOTOGRAPHY BY ARTIST

NANCY NEARING
Trumpet Bead ■ 2012
5.1 x 2 x 2 cm
Polymer clay, brass cap; cane work
PHOTOGRAPHY BY ARTIST

1000
beads

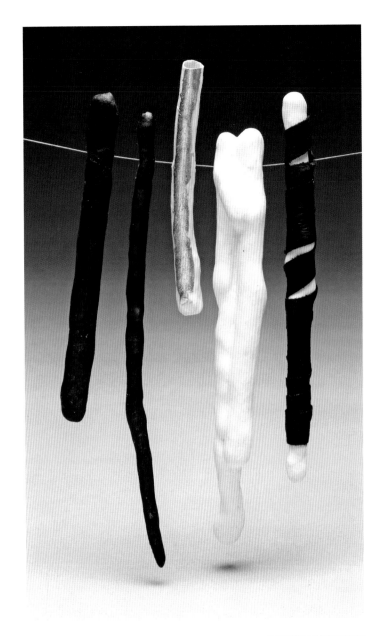

BONNIE LAMBERT
Twigs ▣ 2011
14 x 0.5 x 0.5 cm
Porcelain, paper, gold foil, leather, paint; fired
PHOTOGRAPHY BY TOM FERRIS

TERRI CASPARY SCHMIDT
Leaf Study No. 2 ▣ 2013
4.5 x 2 x 2 cm
Soda-lime glass; lampworked, etched
PHOTOGRAPHY BY MARGOT GEIST

SUZANNE EVON
Handmade Bead Number 2 ■ 2012
Each: 0.8 x 4 x 0.8 cm
Sterling silver, 18-karat gold
vermeil; oxidized, fabricated
PHOTOGRAPHY BY JEANNE RHODES-MOEN

SO YOUNG PARK
Flower ■ 2012
15 x 15 x 1.5 cm
Silver, 24-karat yellow gold leaf, freshwater pearls;
oxidized, hand fabricated, hammered, soldered
PHOTOGRAPHY BY ARTIST

SALLY CRAIG
Tassel Necklace ■ 2012
45.8 x 2.5 x 2.5 cm
22-karat gold drum beads, 18-karat gold drum beads, silver drum beads,
sterling silver, 18-karat gold; oxidized, hand woven and fabricated
PHOTOGRAPHY BY RALPH GABRINER

J.C. HERRELL
Silver Construct Prism Bead ■ 2013
4.2 x 2.6 x 2.6 cm
Soda-lime glass, enamel, silver foil;
lampworked, stringer work
PHOTOGRAPHY BY ARTIST

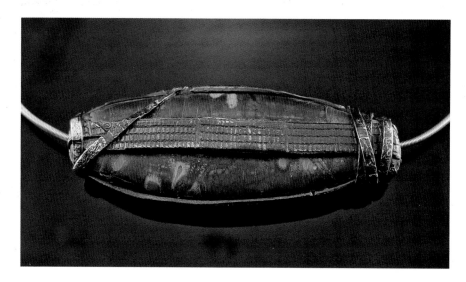

LYDIA MUELL
Scorpio Moon ■ 2013
2.5 x 2.5 x 1 cm
Glass; dichroic layering
PHOTOGRAPHY BY ARTIST

LOUISE LITTLE
Desert Artifact ■ 2011
3.2 x 7 x 0.9 cm
Soda-lime glass, metal clay;
lampworked, etched, embellished
PHOTOGRAPHY BY ARTIST

LISA ATCHISON
Electroformed Leaf Bead ■ 2012
5.6 x 2.8 x 1.5 cm
Soda-lime glass, silver, maple leaf, copper;
flameworked, fumed, electroformed
PHOTOGRAPHY BY ARTIST

SALLY PRASCH
Copper Core ■ 2013
1.5 x 1.5 x 1.5 cm
Borosilicate glass; flameworked
PHOTOGRAPHY BY MIKE BRANDT

GALINA GREBENNIKOVA
Forest Nymph ■ 2012
2.5 x 2.5 x 2.5 cm
Wool, copper, glass pearls, seed beads;
hand felted, cut, formed
PHOTOGRAPHY BY ARTIST

LAURIE NESSEL
Mosaic Ocean ■ 2012
4.3 x 4.9 x 4.9 cm
Soda-lime glass, silver leaf; flameworked, cane work, acid etched
PHOTOGRAPHY BY ARTIST

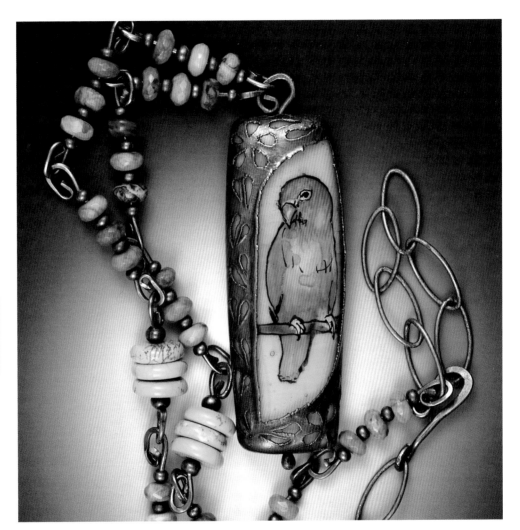

VICKIE HALLMARK
Retro Lovebird ■ 2009

6.3 x 2.5 x 1.2 cm
Glass, enamel, copper; flameworked, reverse painted, fused, electroformed
PHOTOGRAPHY BY ARTIST

VICKIE HALLMARK
White Lovebird ■ 2009
6.3 x 2 x 1.3 cm
Glass, enamel, copper; flameworked,
reverse painted, fused, electroformed
PHOTOGRAPHY BY ARTIST

CAROL MARANDO
Portrait Bead ■ 2011
3.5 x 3.7 x 3.7 cm
Soda-lime glass; flameworked, murrini
PHOTOGRAPHY BY JULIE BOLAND

LORETTA LAM
Heart of Gold ■ 2012

51 x 2.8 x 1.8 cm
Polymer beads, coconut spacers, mokume
gane; millefiori, Skinner blend
PHOTOGRAPHY BY ARTIST

ALICE KRESSE
Carbon Beads ■ 2013

Each: 2.5 x 2.5 cm
Wood beads, black spinel, cubic zirconia, freshwater
pearls, sterling silver; fired, burned, set, drilled, dapped
PHOTOGRAPHY BY ARTIST

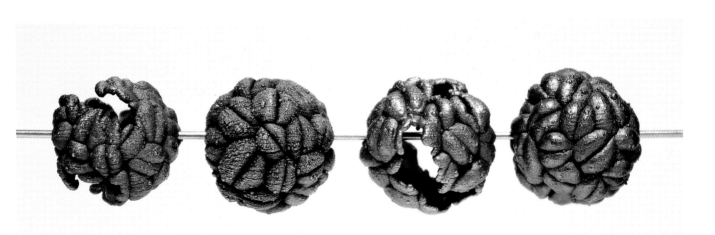

EMMA GERARD
Growth and Decay ■ 2012

Each: 2.5 x 2.5 x 2.5 cm
Copper, patina; electroformed
PHOTOGRAPHY BY ARTIST

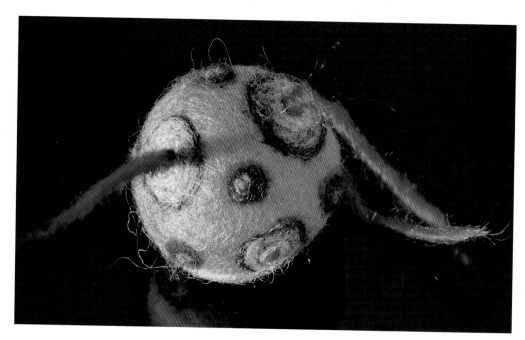

DEBORAH CONTI
Peach Fuzzz ■ 2013
13 x 13 x 5 cm
Dryer lint, recycled wool roving; dyed, needlefelted
PHOTOGRAPHY BY STEPHEN W. LONG

KARI LINDSAY-BEALE
Fireball ■ 2010
3 x 5 x 5 cm
Glass; flameworked, blown, flame sculpted
PHOTOGRAPHY BY BIRGIT PHOTOGRAPHY

HEATHER BEHRENDT
Glowing Crystals ■ 2013

Each: 1.6 x 1.5 x 1.5 cm
Soda-lime glass; flameworked, encased, acid etched
PHOTOGRAPHY BY ARTIST

JUDITH KAUFMAN
Pearl Necklace ■ 2009

17 x 0.8 x 0.8 cm
Tahitian pearls, diamonds, 22-karat
yellow gold, 18-karat green gold
PHOTOGRAPHY BY HAP SAKWA

BARBARA LIVENSTEIN
Untitled ■ 2010

Largest bead: 3.2 cm in diameter
Sterling silver, 22-karat gold; hollow constructed,
planished, textured, married metal

AIMEE MILAN
Ambrogio ■ 2013

2.4 x 3.3 cm
Soda-lime glass, silver leaf,
sterling silver tube, brass spacers;
flameworked, metalwork

AMY KAROLY
Sweet Little Birdhouse ■ 2013
2 x 1.5 x 1.5 cm
Copper precious metal clay; sculpted,
carved, constructed
PHOTOGRAPHY BY ARTIST

LESLIE FORD
Untitled ■ 2013
3.2 x 2.9 x 2.9 cm
Glass, copper, silver, brass;
flameworked, capped, cored
PHOTOGRAPHY BY ARTIST

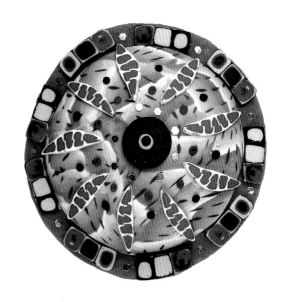

BONNIE LAMBERT
Sycamore ■ 2011

Dimensions vary
Sycamore pods, gold foil
PHOTOGRAPHY BY TOM FERRIS

DAYLE DOROSHOW
Fruit Burst ■ 2012

2 x 2 x 1 cm
Polymer clay; millefiori
PHOTOGRAPHY BY ARTIST

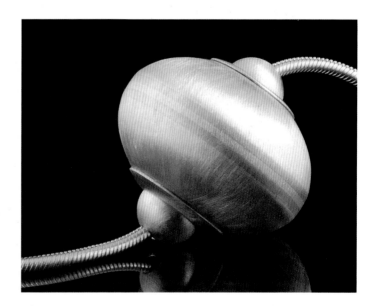

SASHA CASE
Kimono Dream Bead ▪ 2013
2.5 x 2.5 x 2.5 cm
Precious metal clay, fine silver sterling
chain, black sapphires, Austrian crystal
beads; cut, syringe technique
PHOTOGRAPHY BY ARTIST

N. KAY MORRISON
Silken Stripes ▪ 2011
2 x 2 x 1.3 cm
Sterling silver, copper-based alloy; hand
fabricated, sawn, dapped, cold connected
PHOTOGRAPHY BY ARTIST

SUZANNE KUSTNER
Nine Gold Beads ■ 2012

Squares: 1 x 1 x 0.5 cm each
Circles: 1 x 0.5 cm each
Triangles: 1 x 1 x 1 cm each
14-karat gold, enamel; cloisonné

NATALIE MARAS
Lichen beads ■ 2013

Each bead: 4 x 4 x 1 cm
Polymer clay, copper leaf;
formed, inlaid, appliquéd
PHOTOGRAPHY BY ARTIST

NADIA TASCI
Klimt Bead ■ 2013
3.2 x 1.7 x 1.7 cm
Soda-lime glass, 22-karat
gold leaf; flameworked
PHOTOGRAPHY BY UROS JELIC

MARION MARSHALL
Golden Om ■ 2010
2.2 x 2.2 x 2.2 cm
18-karat yellow gold, sterling silver; fabricated
PHOTOGRAPHY BY ARTIST

MILLI JEWELL ■ 2012
Golden Lentils

Each: 1.3 x 1.3 x 0.5 cm
Polymer clay, Swarovski crystals; mica shift
PHOTOGRAPHY BY ARTIST

N. KAY MORRISON
Orbital Weave ■ 2011

2.2 x 2.2 x 1.3 cm
Sterling silver, copper; hand fabricated,
textured, sawn, dapped, cold connected
PHOTOGRAPHY BY ARTIST

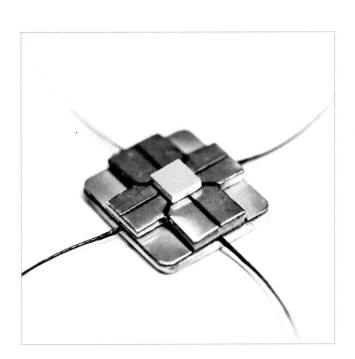

HESTER POPMA-VAN DE KOLK
Wearable Home Bead ■ 2012

1 x 1.2 x 0.3 cm
Plastic bits from SIM cards, credit
cards, and telephone cards
PHOTOGRAPHY BY ARTIST

GWEN FISHER
Pentagon and Square Links ■ 2013

Each: 1 x 1 x 0.3 cm
Metal and glass seed beads, Swarovski crystal,
thread; embellished cubic right-angle weave
PHOTOGRAPHY BY ARTIST

KATHERINE WADSWORTH
Vetro Blue Blossom Necklace ■ 2012
Largest bead: 2.8 x 2.5 cm
Glass, silver metal clay; lampworked, etched, sculpted
PHOTOGRAPHY BY BRAD MOON

TOP
ANNE DONZÉ
Rosée ■ 2012

2.5 x 6.5 x 1 cm
Sterling silver, blown glass; flameworked
PHOTOGRAPHY BY ARTIST

BOTTOM
TAMMY WOLTER
Borosilicate Glass + Electricity + Copper! ■ 2012

Left: 2.5 x 2 cm; center: 3 x 1.5 cm; right: 2 x 2 cm
Glass; flameworked, electroformed
PHOTOGRAPHY BY DAVID ORR

BECKY FAIRCLOUGH
Urban Butterfly ■ 2010

3.7 x 1.7 x 0.6 cm
Soda-lime glass, enamels, lusters,
cubic zirconias; flameworked
PHOTOGRAPHY BY ARTIST

SANDRA BORNEMANN
Turquoise Dots ◼ 2012
2.5 x 2.8 x 2.5 cm
Soda-lime glass, handmade silver
bead caps; flameworked

NANCY NEARING
Bird and Lotus ◼ 2013
3.1 x 2.5 x 2.5 cm
Polymer clay, copper, glass; cane work, modeled

JACQUELINE KELLER
Leona ■ 2011
4 x 1.7 x 1.7 cm
Soda-lime glass, silver glass
PHOTOGRAPHY BY ARTIST

PENNY DICKINSON
Encased Floral Beads ■ 2012
Each: 1.9 x 1.3 x 1.3 cm
Italian glass, opaque frit; flameworked
PHOTOGRAPHY BY DAVID ORR

AMANDA MUDDIMER
Folklore Collection ■ 2013

Each bead: 1.5 x 1.5 x 1.5 cm
Soda-lime glass; flameworked
PHOTOGRAPHY BY PENNY OLIVER

contributing artists

Albright, Tristyn
York, Pennsylvania 154

Anderson, Michou Pascale
Hamburg, Germany 200

Arden, Kimberly
Temperance, Michigan 161, 264

Armstrong, Jessica
Midway, Kentucky 81

Atchison, Lisa
Indianapolis, Indiana 92, 262, 391

Bachmann, Karen
Brooklyn, New York 295, 378

Backer, Vanessa
San Diego, California 27, 146

Baldwin, Doug
Prescott, Arizona 182

Ballard, Amber
Iron Ridge, Wisconsin 107, 382

Banner, Maureen
Monterey, Massachusetts 38

Banner, Michael
Monterey, Massachusetts 38

Barrett, Beau
Port Townsend, Washington 115, 279, 326

Barrett, Dolores
Camarillo, California 58, 95, 384

Behrendt, Heather
Walworth, London, England 358, 399

Bellamy, Sherry
Maple Ridge, British Columbia, Canada 179, 336

Berman, Sher
Deerfield, Illinois 213

Bernbaum, Marta
Brattleboro, Vermont 159

Best, Paula
Rio Rancho, New Mexico 113

Blackburn, Carol
London, England 108, 364

Blankenship, Julie
Mesa, Arizona 324

Bogonovich, Megan
Concord, New Hampshire 70, 212

Bonham, Mags
Bolton, Vermont 141

Bonitz, Kay
Hendersonville, North Carolina 95, 296, 357, 384

Boothe, Anna
Zieglerville, Pennsylvania 368

Bornemann, Sandra
Bromham, Bedfordshire, England 75, 281, 413

Bourke, Emma
Westport, County Mayo, Ireland 184

Bowker, Laura
Stanwood, Washington 156

Boyer, Ivy
Phoenix, Arizona 310

Breyter, Paula
Buenos Aires, Argentina 266

Broome, Tracey
Chapel Hill, North Carolina 250

Brown, Amy
East Lansing, Michigan 199

Burke, Shauna
Brooklyn, New York 53

Burns, Nell
North Vancouver, British Columbia, Canada 227

Butler, Lauren
Cessnock, New South Wales, Australia 359

Buyum, Nofar
Tel Aviv, Israel 63

Cahill, Patti
Mars Hill, North Carolina 300

Cain, Nancy
Colorado Springs, Colorado 102

Case, Sasha
Tucson, Arizona 299, 404

Caspary Schmidt, Terri
Albuquerque, New Mexico 287, 325, 328, 387

Castano, Aurelio
White Plains, New York 214, 289

Chelminsky, Dania
Tel Aviv, Israel 145, 363

Cheong, Sunyoung
Topeka, Kansas 59

Chin, Maureen
Cary, North Carolina 182

Clements, Jemma
Hobart, Tasmania, Australia 274

Colby, Betsy
Shelter Island Heights, New York, 273

Coletti, Michele
Phoenix, Arizona 233

Conti, Deborah
Satellite Beach, Florida 398

Cooney, Harold
Longmont, Colorado 37, 119, 153

Cooper, Holly
Austin, Texas 137, 274, 355, 360

Craig, Sally
Amherst, Massachusetts 389

Daamen, Brigit
Haarlem, Netherlands 228

Dagan, Ronit
Herzliya, Israel 257, 329

Davies, Christine
Birmingham, England 90

de Diego, Miguel
Seville, Spain 260

Delarue, Marion
Carbon-Blanc, France 60, 204

Dewison, Caroline
Warrington, Cheshire, England 105

Di Francesco, Carla
Stuttgart, Germany 370

Dias, Cristina
Brooklyn, New York 242

DiCarlo, Courtney
Athens, Georgia 26, 277, 297

Dickinson, Penny
Peoria, Arizona 374, 414

Dintenfass, Phyllis
Appleton, Wisconsin 318

DiPiazza, Tracy
Belleview, Missouri 194, 240

Donzé, Anne
Crozet, France 411

Doroshow, Dayle
Fort Bragg, California 12, 328, 403

Dowding, Valeria
Buenos Aires, Argentina 258

Dudley, Janel
Grants Pass, Oregon 204

Duggan, Patrick
Summer Hill, New South Wales, Australia 343

Dummer, Kathryn
Columbus, Ohio 132

Dunbar, Annie
Sunnyvale, California 113

Durrwachter Rushing, Darlene
Pittsburgh, Pennsylvania 45

Duval, Muriel
Laval, Quebec, Canada 143, 155

Edeiken, Linda
San Diego, California 112

Eder, Katharina
Mödling, Austria 41

Edöcs, Marta
Sopron, Hungary 130, 186

Edwards, Kim
Bloomery, West Virginia 122

Egholt, Tove
Stockholm, Sweden 314

Einav, Galit
Rishon Le-Zion, Israel 62, 136, 218

Ellenton, Susan
Victoria, British Columbia, Canada 51, 147

Engel, Mary
Athens, Georgia 26, 277, 297

Eriksen Mapp, Hanne
Paraparaumu, Kapiti Coast, New Zealand 105

Evans-Paige, Debra
Le Sueur, Minnesota 204

Evins, Patsy
Hallettsville, Texas 192

Evon, Suzanne
Weaverville, North Carolina 388

Fairclough, Becky
Chilworth, Surrey, England 237, 381, 412

Fajardo, Barbara
Albuquerque, New Mexico 31, 260

Faulkner, Jonna
Escondido, California 270, 312

acknowledgments

Thank you to Julie Hale for her support, her kind approach, and her talent with the written word. Thanks also to former Lark editor Ray Hemachandra for his phone call asking me to be a part of this project and for all the professional phone calls we shared over the years.

I'm indebted to all of the artists—not just the ones included in this book—who are making beads today. I send my heartfelt thanks to all of you. I feel fortunate to be a part of a your community.

—Kristina Logan
(Kristina's work is featured on this page.)

Sophia Necklace ■ 2009
PHOTOGRAPHY BY DEAN POWELL

Floral Glass Beads ■ 2013
PHOTOGRAPHY BY DEAN POWELL

Ancient Glass Beads ■
FROM THE JUROR'S PERSONAL COLLECTION

about the juror

Kristina Logan is recognized internationally for her glass beads. She was one of only four artists selected for the Smithsonian American Art Museum's 2002 exhibition "The Renwick Invitational: Four Discoveries in Craft." Articles about her work have appeared in *Beadwork* magazine, *Lapidary Journal*, and *La Revue de la Céramique et du Verre*. Kristina has taught beadmaking at a number of prestigious schools, including The Studio of the Corning Museum of Glass in Corning, New York; the Penland School of Crafts in Penland, North Carolina; the Musée-Atelier du Verre in Sars-Poteries, France; and Centro Studio Vetro and Abate Zanetti in Venice, Italy. Kristina served as president of the International Society of Glass Beadmakers from 1996 to 1998. Her work is in collections around the world, including those of the Smithsonian American Art Museum's Renwick Gallery, the Corning Museum of Glass, and the Musée-Atelier du Verre. Kristina lives in Portsmouth, New Hampshire.